Happy Birthday Morag

I'll let you try the recipes first !!

love from

Ronnie

Feb 1996.

ENTERTAINING
WITH
FOOD
AND
DRINK

ENTERTAINING
WITH
FOOD
AND
DRINK

MICHAEL BARRY
and
JILLY GOOLDEN

Photographs by
TIM HILL

BBC BOOKS

Thanks are due to many people who have thought, spoken, eaten and digested on behalf of this book, and particularly to Orla Broderick who has done all of these things with particular skill and dedication.

M . B .

Published by BBC Books,
an imprint of BBC Worldwide Publishing,
BBC Worldwide Limited, Woodlands,
80 Wood Lane, London W12 0TT

First published 1995

ISBN: 0 563 37149 8

Designed by Roger Daniels
Styling by Zoë Hill
Home Economist Simon Collins

Set in Sabon and News Gothic by Selwood Systems,
Midsomer Norton
Printed and bound in Great Britain by Butler & Tanner Ltd, Frome
Colour separations by Radstock Reproductions Ltd,
Midsomer Norton

Jacket printed by Lawrence Allen Ltd, Weston-super-Mare

Page 2: *Smoked Salmon Fingers* (see page 166)

CONTENTS

Notes on the Recipes

You can use this book as a conventional source of recipe ideas for starters, main courses and desserts by referring to the Recipe Index by Course on page 220.

Recipes suitable for vegetarians are marked with a (V) symbol. These recipes may contain cheese and other dairy products.

The shopping trolley symbol 🛒 indicates a crafty shopping tip. When the symbol is used within a recipe, a page reference is given for the details (unless the tip is on the same page). The crafty tips which come after the menus give advice on those dishes that can be prepared in advance and/or frozen.

Follow one set of measurements only. Do not mix metric and imperial.

Eggs are size 2. Government advice is still not to eat raw eggs. This is particularly important for children, pregnant women, older people and the infirm. Healthy adults may wish to make up their own minds.

Spoon measurements are level.

It's possible to adjust seasoning and strongly-flavoured ingredients, such as onions and garlic, to suit your taste.

Usually, if you substitute freeze-dried for fresh herbs, use only half the amount specified.

FAN OVENS AND AGAS

All the recipes in this book can be cooked in an Aga or fan oven. Of course, each requires a rather different approach to cooking. As a guide, for fan ovens reduce the temperature by 20C (36F). For Agas, use the bottom of the roasting oven for gas mark 4, 180C (350F). Use the top of the oven for higher temperatures, and the slow oven for lower temperatures.

INTRODUCTIONS

FOOD

Entertaining, for me, is a word that covers a multitude of pleasures. Sometimes it's a little dish for two, what the French would call a *bonne bouche*, to give my wife a treat. It may involve having the whole family at home for a special occasion, a feast or just a family get together. It can be a formal dinner party, something knocked up from the fridge when friends happen to drop round, a wedding breakfast for a hundred or a picnic for two. The key point about cooking for entertaining is that it should be for pleasure, not just for nourishment. In fact, when I think about it, I very rarely cook just for nourishment, so perhaps all my cooking is really about entertaining, and that includes entertaining myself.

However pleasurable cooking can be it sometimes becomes a chore and that is what this book is about – making sure that when you do your entertaining you get as much of the pleasure and as few of the chores as possible. Over the years I have found that my approach to entertaining has changed quite a lot and I hope that in this book I can share with you some of the thoughts and ideas I have developed with some of the discoveries I have made.

We modern cooks have a lot going for us. I know it is

fashionable to complain about processed foods and vegetables grown for looks not flavour, but the fact of the matter is that we now have at our disposal an enviable range of foods, techniques, equipment and technology.

So the idea behind this book is to make entertaining easy with real convenience food cooked fast, making use of the extraordinary range of resources that are available to us. All the dishes are designed to be cooked in under 45 minutes, from scratch, unless otherwise stated. Obviously, you will need to cook your chosen accompaniments at the same time.

The first chapter in this book contains some basic recipes, techniques and methods that can be used in a variety of dishes or meals. The recipes are really simple, but can be endlessly adapted – one of the secrets of cooking, crafty and otherwise.

But to begin at the beginning of all entertaining, let's go shopping. I can remember, for instance, when olive oil in Britain was something sold in chemists' as a pharmaceutical product – literally: Olive Oil B.P. Last week in my local, admittedly large, urban, supermarket I counted no fewer than seventeen different olive oils ranging from extra virgin, cold pressed organic from Portugal through six other countries of origin and three flavour variations of an olive and sunflower oil mix. That extraordinary variety is a product of our amazingly expanded, sophisticated tastes, consumer pressure (well done, us!) and the imagination of the retailers that has made British supermarkets and speciality shops such a delight to shop in.

Except on extra special occasions, I would rarely make the tomato *sugo* or sauce for a pasta dish and that is especially true if I have lunch for twelve or more! I can buy one called Sugo Casa which has added to it some dried tomato paste, fresh basil and olive oil and it is certainly a match for the sauce that previously would have taken nearly forty minutes to make from scratch. In a market in Singapore I remember watching amazed as a woman who had bought a head of garlic had it peeled, trimmed and ground to a paste for her as part of the service. You can buy the equivalent now in jars for less than £1 with only a little vegetable oil added as a preservative. You can also buy fresh ginger, lemon grass and fresh hot chillies all similarly ground and prepared ready for use. These products are wonderful ingredients with most of the hard work taken out. You will find I make good use of them in this book and I have provided you with all the information you need to buy them.

Also a blessing are the prepared meats and vegetables that

can transform ordinary dishes into special occasions. There are boned chicken breasts, turkey escalopes, scrubbed and prepared mushrooms, fresh packed trimmed mangetout and baby sweet-corn all ready-to-cook, salad mixtures and peeled fresh pineapple in its own juice – just to skim over the ingredients still waiting for your skill and enthusiasm. Here then is crafty cooking based on a cornucopia from every corner of the globe. This book makes use of lots of these materials and others, too. Pre-baked savoury, sweet and herbed pastry shells are a prime example. But this is not a packet sauce or canned soup book. All soups and most sauces are simple to make, especially when using the crafty techniques.

I'm delighted to have as my collaborator, once more, Jilly Goolden. Jilly has contributed all the drinks advice and ideas to this book.

Michael Barry

WINE

As far as I'm concerned, wine is itself entertaining, as well as being an accessory to entertainment.

And I'm not speaking as a lush, but as a taster. There is a wider spectrum of flavours offered by wine than by any other single source of food or drink that I can think of. One thousand different grape varieties can be used to make wine in more than forty different countries. The flavour spectrum is like a rainbow; it's impossible to get to the end of it.

I'm frequently asked which is my favourite wine and I have to answer that it's as often as not whatever I have in my glass at the time. Undoubtedly for me variety is the thing. A great deal of pleasure lies in the quest for the new and the different. I'm not hung up on history and nor am I especially impressed by labels. For me taste beats pedigree every time. When you are choosing wines for entertaining, don't feel you have to break the bank and go for a classic name. If you buy a wine you like, the chances are the taste will impress your guests as well.

People who don't know me very well often imagine that we serve rich and rare bottles when we have friends around at home. And they couldn't be further from the truth!

'Unassuming little numbers' are more to the point, inexpensive wines that are chosen to give your tastebuds a thrill. I certainly don't stock up on the best vintages from the classic areas, but instead buy what takes my fancy on the day. If you have stocks of case after case of the same wine, the trouble is that you have to drink it even if you would prefer to have something else. No, heretical though it may sound, I don't favour the 'laying down' approach (except in exceptional circumstances, such as inexpensive champagne, which benefits from a few months lying quietly under the stairs).

High street wine shops, wine merchants and supermarkets have their shelves stacked with bottles ready to drink now. I like to check them out, look closely at the price tags and swoop on the most interesting – often the best priced – buy; take it home, if it's white encourage it to achieve quickly the correct temperature, open, pour and enjoy. There's infinite pleasure to be taken from discovering brilliant, with luck inexpensive, finds and sharing them with friends. That's how wine continues to be entertaining as well as enhancing many forms of social entertainment.

Jilly Goolden

1

CRAFTY BASIC RECIPES

A quick trip around the supermarket these days and you're spoiled for choice. On top of that, supermarkets now offer free leaflets and cards giving their own recipe ideas, suggested menus, advice on safety etc.

But how can you turn all this into meals for your own table? With which utensil do you make which sauce to go with which kind of pasta? How can you prepare a whole meal at a moment's notice? Confused? You needn't be. The crafty guide to effortless entertaining starts here.

THE FOOD PROCESSOR

The fundamental tool of the modern kitchen is the food processor. It helps with all kinds of vegetable and meat preparation, for salads, pâtés and terrines, carnivorous or vegetarian. It even makes great pastry if you don't fancy ready-made pastry shells or ready-to-roll pastry, frozen or fresh. The first thing to remember about a food processor is that it really needs to be treated like a knife. That means it is a basic everyday kitchen tool and needs to be kept ready to use at any time out of its box, on the work surface, plugged in ready to go. I find that I use the processor for a whole range of things from chopping up big handfuls of parsley to puréeing soup, and as casually as I might use a knife to slice a tomato. Don't be put off by the washing up as there is only ever the bowl, lid and blade, none of which takes much more than a quick wipe.

The second thing to do is to find out what the machine will and won't do. Modern food processors will, for example, whip eggs very efficiently whereas the earlier ones didn't. Some come with an added liquidiser or other attachments which make them even more flexible. So it is worth experimenting, particularly with cheap foods like a couple of potatoes, to see how it will slice, shred and grate, and what difference is made by the variable speed, which many of them now possess.

A couple of safety points – most of the blades are very sharp, particularly the basic working tool, the double-bladed knife. It is important when you are using it to make sure you have removed it from the bowl before you pour out anything you have been processing, otherwise the blade can fall out and give you a very nasty cut. The slicer blades are often very sharp, too, and need careful handling, so do be very careful when washing up.

THE MICROWAVE

Another very useful tool in my repertoire of crafty techniques, comes the microwave. I've always been suspicious about some of the claims for these little white boxes.

'Oven' is a word they only justify, for example, with the arrival of the third generation (now widely available at reasonable prices) that include the real feature of ovens – radiant and circulated heat. These are a wonderful boon for hastening cooking as they produce browned, sealed food cooked in incredibly short times, thanks to the microwave facility. As all these new ovens differ slightly I've not given times or specific methods for them. One last thought on microwave cooking – if you have staggered timings for meals, the microwave oven does heat food up quicker and better than anything I know. So don't just use them for making baked potatoes – I beg you.

Mayonnaise

MAKES ABOUT 250 ML/8 FL OZ

Home-made mayonnaise is the easiest thing in the world and you can make it in just a few minutes. You can easily ring the changes by varying the oils and flavourings, herbs and spices. As well as a food processor you can also make mayonnaise in a liquidiser using almost exactly the same technique. Liquidisers tend to run at a rather higher speed, though, so you may need to process it for a shorter period of time. This, by the way, is whole egg mayonnaise, similar in style to 'American' mayonnaise. If you want the thicker, softer, more golden style substitute three egg yolks for the whole egg. Whichever version you make, the egg(s) must be really fresh.

1 egg (size 3), at room temperature
1 tbsp lemon juice
½ tsp salt
½ tsp sugar
1 tsp French mustard
175 ml/6 fl oz oil (ideally a mixture of olive oil and sunflower to your taste)

Carefully break the egg into the mixing bowl with the double-edged blade in place. Add the lemon juice, salt, sugar and mustard and a quarter of the oil. Secure the lid and turn on to maximum speed for 10 seconds. Allow to stand for a couple of seconds. Turn on again at medium speed and pour the remaining oil through the feed tube at the top of the processor in a thin steady stream with the engine running. As the oil meets the mayonnaise it will gradually thicken until it becomes as smooth and thick as you want. This should take about 25–30 seconds. Stop the machine, take the lid off, scrape down the sides, and process again for 2–3 seconds. Place in a jar or bowl, cover with clingfilm and chill. It will keep for up to one week.

VARIATION:
Aïoli: Add two peeled garlic cloves to the egg, lemon juice, salt, sugar and mustard mixture and process until the garlic is thoroughly puréed. Add the oil and proceed as above.

OLIVE OIL
The delight in using olive oil lies in the fact that it is not a standardised product. It ranges in colour and taste from pale gold and delicate to dark green and fruity. Look for cold pressed olive oil, especially extra virgin oil which has a low acidity (1 per cent or less) followed by virgin which has a maximum of 2 per cent. Any olive oil labelled 'pure' is 'refined' which means that it has been stripped of its character after a third or fourth pressing. 'Light' is produced by the fifth pressing and has a mild flavour.

My favourite is the golden, fragrant oil from Greece, but it has to be said that savouring the taste of olive oils from different countries is one of life's joys. Try it and see – it will add a whole new dimension to your cooking.

FRENCH MUSTARD
Real French mustard comes in three main varieties: Bordeaux, darkish-brown and rather spicy; Meaux, from the Burgundy area and also known as l'Ancienne, which is crunchy and has very visible texture in it; and Dijon, also from the Burgundy region, pale gold, and often surprisingly pungent, though never as hot as English mustard. When faced with a shelf of mustards choose the French branded versions.

White Wine or Cider Vinegar Vinaigrette

MAKES ABOUT 300 ML/½ PINT

This is a lighter dressing particularly suitable for white vegetables like cauliflower, or for potato salad. It also benefits in pungency from the addition of the mustard. If you do not have any grapeseed oil, 250 ml/8 fl oz of sunflower oil will work just as well.

4 tbsp white wine or cider vinegar
1 tsp Dijon mustard **(see page 15)**
½ tsp salt
½ tsp sugar
50 ml/2 fl oz grapeseed oil
175 ml/6 fl oz sunflower oil

Mix the vinegar, mustard, salt and sugar together until the salt and sugar are thoroughly dissolved. Add the grapeseed and sunflower oils and blend or shake until thoroughly mixed.

WINE AND CIDER VINEGARS

All vinegar is made from modified alcohol – such as beer (for malt vinegar), cider or wine. The strength and subtlety of the vinegars usually reflect their point of origin. You can get sherry and champagne vinegars and others flavoured with fruit and herbs. Except for pickling, avoid malt vinegar and use one of the other lighter versions. Balsamic vinegar is wonderfully dark and mellow, with a strong sweet-sour flavour, and is only made in and around Modena in Northern Italy. It is expensive but a little goes a long way – just a drop or two with some extra virgin olive oil makes an excellent salad dressing.

Red Wine Vinaigrette

MAKES ABOUT 300 ML/½ PINT

This is the great southern French dressing, wonderful on thick sun-ripened tomatoes in salads. But I enjoy this version with green salads as well, and particularly those made with the slightly bitter lettuces like frisée or endive . As with all vinaigrettes the order of mixing is very important because sugar and salt do not dissolve properly once the oil is added. You can use either all olive or sunflower oil if you choose. If using with tomatoes or other vegetables, an hour or so marinating in the dressing greatly improves the flavour, but for green salads, dress within ten minutes of eating.

4 tbsp red wine vinegar
½ tsp salt
½ tsp sugar
50 ml/2 fl oz olive oil **(see page 15)**
175 ml/6 fl oz sunflower oil

Mix the vinegar, salt and sugar together until the salt and sugar are thoroughly dissolved, whether you are using a processor or shaking in a jar. Add the olive oil and process or shake again and then add the sunflower oil. Make sure the dressing is thoroughly blended.

FRISEE AND ENDIVE LETTUCE

These are confusing names because we use them for different things from the French and Belgians. Frisée literally means frizzy and in the UK is the kind of lettuce that looks as though it has had its leaves shredded. Endive is a lettuce-like plant that has slightly thick and fleshy leaves and a slightly bitter, chicory flavour. Both are great for winter salads.

Herb Vinaigrette

MAKES ABOUT 350 ML/12 FL OZ

This is a particularly nice dressing for salads made of delicate vegetables like French beans or cherry tomatoes or for use on rice or pasta salads. It does not keep as well as the other dressings in this chapter and should be used within three or four days. Finely chop the herbs so that they will be suspended in the dressing.

50 ml/2 fl oz lemon juice
50 ml/2 fl oz white wine or cider vinegar 🛒 (see opposite)
½ tsp salt
½ tsp sugar
2 tsp finely chopped fresh parsley or ½ tsp freeze-dried parsley 🛒 (see page 53)
2 tsp finely chopped chives or ½ tsp freeze-dried chives 🛒 (see page 53)
2 tsp finely chopped basil or ½ tsp freeze-dried basil 🛒 (see page 53)
250 ml/8 fl oz sunflower or light vegetable oil

Put the lemon juice, wine or cider vinegar, salt, sugar and herbs together and process or shake until the salt and sugar are dissolved. Add the oil and process or shake again.

VINAIGRETTES
Known the world over as French dressing, vinaigrettes are very easy to make and can be used in many ways. They are probably best made in a food processor or liquidiser, because the machine emulsifies the dressing so that the oil, vinegar and flavourings are well mixed. But you can also put the ingredients in a jar or bottle with a secure top and just shake it thoroughly until the dressing is well mixed. It will separate more quickly than if made in a processor but can always be shaken again. With the exception of the Herb Vinaigrette, all of these dressings will keep in the fridge, for a week or more, in a sealed jar and indeed, there is a view that they improve slightly if kept for a day or two as the flavours are given longer to infuse.

Lemonette Dressing

MAKES ABOUT 350 ML/12 FL OZ

This is a dressing from the Middle East where lemon juice is used entirely to replace vinegar as the acidic flavouring in the dressing. It tends to be used in composite salads like tabbouleh (a mixture of parsley, mint, spring onions and cracked wheat – see page 94), or as a dressing over lentils or other pulses, and is very good with a bean salad (see page 174). I like it best on a Greek salad – a mixture of crisp lettuce, cherry tomatoes, black olives and feta cheese (see page 53). The lemon seems to bring out the flavour of all the other ingredients. Use fresh lemon juice if you can for this recipe; the flavour really does make a difference.

½ tsp salt
1 tsp sugar
100 ml/4 fl oz fresh lemon juice
50 ml/2 fl oz olive oil 🛒 (see page 15)
175 ml/6 fl oz sunflower or light vegetable oil

Dissolve the salt and sugar in the lemon juice, add the olive oil and shake thoroughly or process. Add the remaining oil and process or shake until the mixture is thoroughly emulsified.

PASTA COOKING

Crafty ways to cook pasta may seem unlikely at first but they work wonderfully well. I ought to add that they were developed when pasta still came to us in the dried form only. Nowadays we can buy fresh, that is soft, pastas which cook in 3 to 4 minutes needing no crafty technique to speed them up. However, they are not always available and the dried varieties can be kept in the storecupboard ready for those last-minute meals. These crafty methods are still terrifically useful and easy to handle. They are also ideal for those forms of pasta which are not available fresh, particularly the more intricate shapes and, surprisingly, spaghetti itself. There are two techniques here: one for pasta that is meant to be served with a sauce, and the other for the flat pasta, lasagne and cannelloni, which are used in baked dishes.

PASTA SHAPES
A good rule of thumb for choosing a pasta shape is that the thicker the sauce the thinner the pasta. The more complex shapes will pick up and carry quite runny sauces which just slip completely off spaghetti or tagliatelli, so a thick cream sauce is ideal for one of the simple plain pastas, and the ones that look like bows or ears or shells are ideal for thinner sauces that they can fill up with. Look out for all the new types and shapes that are continually coming out on the market, such as ready-rolled cannelloni or lasagnette which is a long, flat pasta with crinkly edges which is three times the width of tagliatelle.

Crafty Method for Dried Pasta

SERVES 4

This works with macaroni, spaghetti, small fusilli, or any dried pasta shapes.

1.75 litres/3 pints water
1 tsp salt
1 tbsp olive oil 🛒 (see page 15)
350 g/12 oz dried pasta shapes 🛒
knob of butter and 1 tbsp olive oil, to serve

Bring the water to the boil in a large saucepan with the lid on. Add the salt and oil and let it come back to the boil. Add the pasta all in one go and stir thoroughly. Return to the boil and boil fast for 3 minutes and switch the heat off. No, really – switch it off completely. Put the lid on the pan. Leave it for between 5–9 minutes depending on how thick the pasta is, less time for thinner pasta, and then drain it through a colander or sieve. Add a knob of butter or a tablespoon of oil and stir quickly to prevent it sticking. The pasta will be perfectly cooked, *al dente* without having gone soggy, and will not require watching like a hawk – a couple of minutes either way while it is resting with the lid on will not make that much difference.

Crafty Method for Flat Pasta

SERVES 4

This works with lasagne and cannelloni. It used to be necessary to cook these pastas for 10 minutes or more before using and they were difficult to handle and separate. This technique makes it very easy to use them either flat or rolled up for stuffing.

It is also possible to buy pre-cooked lasagne and ready-rolled cannelloni. Whether you are using the crafty method, or pre-cooked, you can make lasagne from a standing start to putting it into the oven in about 12 minutes. You will find the beef, or vegetarian, tomato sauce recipe below and the béchamel (white) sauce recipe on page 20.

1.2 litres/2 pints water
1 tsp salt
1 tbsp olive oil 🛒 (see page 15)
350 g/12 oz flat pasta, plus the appropriate
sauces or fillings

Bring the water to the boil, add the salt and oil and return to the boil. Pour into a large flat dish like a baking dish and slide the pasta, sheet by sheet, into the boiling water. It does not need to be reheated at this stage. Allow to soak for 3 minutes and then, if making lasagne, use straight from the water without drying, layering it with the meat and béchamel sauces as you go.
If making cannelloni, allow another 2–3 minutes until the pasta is completely bendable, put a line of the filling down each piece of pasta, roll up, place in the baking dish and cover with sauce. The pasta will cook completely using this method on condition you take it straight from the water and make no attempt to dry it. You may want to make the sauces a little runnier than usual but it is not something to worry about.

Quick Tomato Sauce

MAKES ABOUT 600 ML/1 PINT

The sauce is great on its own with pasta or can have meat or fish, mushrooms or other vegetables added. It can also be the basis of a Mediterranean-style casserole in which the food is cooked very slowly in this sauce, and for making up baked pasta dishes. A couple of tablespoonfuls of double cream stirred in before adding it to pasta creates the authentic richness of Bolognese cooking. Without

the cream the flavouring is more reminiscent of the south of Italy and the Naples region.

2 tbsp olive oil 🛒 (see page 15)
500 ml/18 fl oz *famiglia sugo* 🛒
1–2 tbsp tomato purée
seasoning
1 tbsp fresh, roughly chopped basil or 1 tsp
freeze-dried basil 🛒 (see page 53)
2 tbsp double cream (optional)

Put the olive oil into a pan and heat gently. Add the *sugo*, and stir until heated through. Stir in the tomato purée (2 tablespoons makes a really thick sauce – if you want it runnier only add 1), taste for seasoning and adjust, and just before using or serving add the basil. If you are using cream, add it at the very end.

VARIATIONS
For three delicious alternatives fry 450 g/1 lb minced beef until well browned, or 350 g/12 oz button mushrooms, or 350 g/12 oz peeled cooked prawns for a few moments before adding to the sauce as above.

FAMIGLIA SUGO
Otherwise known as *salsina* or *sugo casa*, this is the perfect sauce base for any number of recipes. Made from fresh crushed tomatoes in thick juice with onions, garlic and herbs added and no artificial ingredients, the flavour is wonderfully rich and it is an excellent short-cut to making a crafty, quick pasta sauce. It is not the same as passata which is sieved tomatoes used as an ingredient for sauces.

Béchamel Sauce

MAKES ABOUT 450 ML/¾ PINT

Béchamel, or white sauce, is one of the most useful sauces in the whole repertoire. You can add all kinds of flavours to it and use it in all sorts of dishes, as I suggest below. The classic way of making it, cooking flour and butter together to make a roux and then adding the liquid bit by bit, requires both time and some skill and, even with both, the sauce can turn out slightly lumpy. Here then is the celebrated crafty white sauce made in a way which is almost foolproof. Use either plain flour or cornflour. Cornflour makes a lighter sauce; the plain flour is best used if you are going to cook something else in the sauce for a long period of time. The standard liquid is milk but you can enrich the sauce by adding cream or make a thinner, lighter sauce by using chicken or vegetable stock (technically, known as velouté). Here are the basic ingredients for a standard white sauce that has the thickness of good double cream.

**450 ml/¾ pint milk (semi-skimmed or full
   cream)**
pinch of salt
40 g/1½ oz plain flour or cornflour
25 g/1 oz butter
a little freshly ground nutmeg

Put the milk into a non-stick pan, add the salt and whisk in the flour using a coil whisk. Cut the butter into pieces, add that to the pan and whisk one more time. Season with nutmeg, place the pan on the heat and bring gently to the boil; this will take about 2–3 minutes. You need to whisk the sauce halfway through and again just before it comes to the boil, whisking it gently but steadily to ensure that it comes to a smooth glossy finish. If you are using cornflour that is all you need to do. If you are using plain flour you will need to continue cooking it for another 2–3 minutes very gently, whisking occasionally.

VARIATIONS
Sauce Mornay (Cheese Sauce)
The best sauces are made with cooking cheeses – the French choice is Gruyère, the English one is Lancashire which has a lovely sharp flavour, and the Italians like Parmesan. Approximately 50 g/2 oz of grated cheese should be stirred into the sauce once it has thickened. The French add a teaspoon of Dijon mustard 🛒 (see page 15), the English a pinch of dried mustard and the Italians another helping of nutmeg.

You can make a French-style fish gratin by pouring the sauce over raw fillets of fish then sprinkling with a little more Gruyère and a few breadcrumbs over the top and baking in a hot oven, 200C/400F/Gas 6/180C fan/top of the Aga, for 25 minutes. Any fish will do but chunky ones like haddock are best.

You might use the Lancashire flavoured cheese sauce to pour over blanched cauliflower (dipped into boiling water, cooked for 1 minute and drained) again to be baked in a moderately hot oven, 190C/375F/Gas 5/175C fan/top of the Aga roasting oven, for 25 minutes. The Italian version with Parmesan and nutmeg is, of course, the perfect addition to lasagne and cannelloni.

Parsley Sauce
Take one recipe of the crafty white sauce and add to it a handful of finely chopped parsley (the food processor does this really well and quickly) and two teaspoons of fresh lemon juice. Stir thoroughly and use with lightly cooked fresh vegetables, poached fish or steamed chicken. Properly made parsley sauce looks really wonderful, pale green in colour with a fresh taste and a surprising lightness.

You can substitute other herbs for the parsley – a handful of snipped fresh chives to dress a savoury dish like chicken is delicious; while fresh green leaves of dill or fennel make a marvellous accompaniment for fish.

Crème Pâtissière (Sweet White Sauce)

MAKES ABOUT 350 ML/12 FL OZ

This marvellous sauce is very easy to make and used for all sorts of things from filling éclairs to providing a sumptuous layer in fancy fruit tarts. It also makes a fabulous trifle. The Italians call trifle, for reasons best known to themselves, English Soup or Zuppa Inglese, and the recipe is given on the right.

150 ml/¼ pint milk
40 g/1½ oz caster sugar
150 ml/¼ pint single cream
25 g/1 oz plain flour
15 g/½ oz cornflour
1 egg, lightly beaten
15 g/½ oz butter

In a heavy-based pan or double boiler, heat the milk and sugar together until the sugar dissolves. Add the cream, flour, cornflour, egg and butter. Whisk over a gentle heat for about 5 minutes until the mixture thickens and just reaches the boil. Do not allow it to boil fast once it starts to bubble or you will wind up with an expensive form of runny scrambled egg. Remove from the heat and allow to cool, whisking occasionally. To avoid the surface forming a skin, put a piece of butter paper or lightly oiled greaseproof paper, that fits the top of the saucepan, butter or oiled side down onto the cooling cream itself.

When it is cold you can use your crème pâtissière for many different purposes or simply decorate the top with cream, using aerosol whipped cream which you can find in any dairy cabinet to achieve professional swirls. (Look for the one with the least sugar.)

Zuppa Inglese

SERVES 4

175 g/6 oz good sponge cake, such as Madeira
5 tbsp fresh orange juice
100 g/4 oz raspberry conserve (see page 36) or jam
200 g/7 oz can peaches in natural juice
150 ml/¼ pint whipping or double cream
350 ml/12 fl oz Crème Pâtissière (see left)
25 g/1 oz toasted flaked almonds
a handful of glacé cherries, quartered

Soak the sponge cake in the orange juice, break it up into walnut-sized chunks and place in the bottom of an attractive glass bowl. Spoon over the raspberry conserve or jam evenly, put the peaches with the juice in a food processor and blend to a smooth purée. Spoon the purée over the cake and jam. Whip the cream until it just holds its shape and then fold into the crème pâtissière. Spread over the peach purée to cover completely. Scatter the almonds and cherries over the crème pâtissière.

FRESH ORANGE JUICE
It is hard to beat the freshly pressed orange juice, which is now readily available in the chill cabinets of shops and supermarkets. (Remember to use it by the date stated on the label otherwise the flavour deteriorates. In fact, the flavour starts to deteriorate after just twenty-four hours). The juice of these oranges is sweeter than those that have had to be picked and ripened in artificial conditions. You can use this juice to make the most wonderful jelly.

FANCY FRENCH SAUCES

The two fancy sauces of classic French cookery are hollandaise and béarnaise. Traditionally they were made with great care by the saucier who was the senior assistant under the head chef of any great kitchen. They are, however, easy-peasy if you have a food processor and know the crafty techniques. Hollandaise sauce is marvellous on things like poached eggs and fish, particularly freshly poached salmon, and it is also used for making classic dishes like *Eggs Benedict* (a layer of toast, a layer of cold cooked tongue, a warm poached egg and then the hollandaise sauce all over the top) – an American invention much to be recommended at brunchtime (see page 104). Béarnaise, on the other hand, a very close relation, is normally used with red meats, particularly with the large entrecôte steak the French classically cook and slice. (If you are feeling flush or fancy a special meal then try it with a properly cooked fillet.) The method for both sauces is similar, but the ingredients differ slightly.

Hollandaise Sauce

MAKES ABOUT 450 ML/¾ PINT

1 egg
2 egg yolks
juice of one lemon
½ tsp salt
225 g/8 oz butter, cut into small pieces

Put the egg, egg yolks, lemon juice and salt in a food processor or a liquidiser and blend until smooth. Gently heat the butter in a heavy-based, non-stick pan until completely melted and foaming. With the motor running at medium speed, pour the butter onto the egg mixture through the feed tube in a continuous thin stream – the sauce will amalgamate and thicken almost immediately. Process for another 5 seconds. Pour it out of the food processor back into the hot pan. Do not return

it to the heat but stir gently for about 30–60 seconds – the heat from the pan will finish the thickening of the sauce. The sauce can be kept hot for about 10 minutes over warm water or in a switched-off but warm oven.

Béarnaise Sauce

MAKES ABOUT 450 ML/¾ PINT

2 tsp tarragon or white wine vinegar 🛒 (see page 16)
1 tsp chopped fresh tarragon
2 egg yolks
1 egg
pinch of salt
225 g/8 oz butter, cut into small pieces

Put the tarragon or white wine vinegar, fresh tarragon, egg yolks and egg into the food processor with the salt. Blend until the tarragon is finely chopped. Gently heat the butter in a heavy-based, non-stick pan until completely melted and foaming. With the motor running at medium speed, pour the butter onto the egg mixture through the feed tube. When the mixture is completely amalgamated, process for another 5 seconds, pour back into the hot pan but do not put on the heat. Allow the heat from the pan to finish thickening the sauce as you stir it gently for another 30–60 seconds before serving. The sauce can be kept hot for about 10 minutes over warm water or in a switched-off but warm oven.

PASTRY

Unfortunately I am not a great pastry maker – I have admitted before to having what is known in the trade as 'hot hands'. However, food processors have rescued me from this personal and irredeemable catastrophe. There is no question that most pastry is best home-made, the one exception being puff pastry, unless, that is, you are a maître pâtissière. Puff pastry, especially in the new, ready-

made vegetarian form, is best bought. Also very
good are the ready-made pastry cases which now
come in a variety of sizes.

Here are two very simple pastries, one savoury
and one sweet.

Savoury Pastry

MAKES ABOUT 400 G/14 OZ

This is suitable for quiches and tarts and, made with
a slightly lower proportion of fat, can be used for
the large, English-style meat pies that used to be
made with hot water pastry. If you want to do that
you will probably need to make it in double quantities
but only add 50 per cent more fat.

225 g/8 oz plain flour
½ tsp salt
150 g/5 oz butter, chilled
1 egg
1 tbsp cold water

Put the flour and salt in the food processor bowl
with the double-bladed knife in place. Cut up the
butter straight from the fridge, into 1 cm/½ in cubes
and add to the bowl. Process at medium speed
until the mixture resembles fine breadcrumbs. With
the motor running, add the egg and allow to blend
into the pastry. Then add half of the water. At
approximately this time the pastry should form a
'ball' around the knife blade and come clean away
from the bowl. If it is still lumpy add the remaining
water. Don't add too much water or the whole thing
will go too soggy. Different flours have different
levels of moisture in them and this is why it is
impossible to be exact. You have to watch for the
balling around the processor blade. As soon as it
happens, take the blade out of the machine, remove
the pastry, give it a couple of pushes with the heel
of your hand to exclude any air bubbles, wrap it in
clingfilm and put it in the fridge for 30 minutes
before using.

Sweet Pastry

MAKES ABOUT 500 G/1¼ LB

This is perfect for all kinds of sweet cooking.

225 g/8 oz plain flour
50 g/2 oz caster sugar
pinch of salt
175 g/6 oz butter, chilled
1 egg
1 tbsp cold water

Put the flour and sugar in a food processor with the
double-bladed knife in place and mix lightly. Add
the salt and the butter, cut into 1 cm/½ in cubes,
straight from the fridge. Process until the whole
mixture resembles fine breadcrumbs. With the
motor running, add the egg through the feed tube
and add half the water. The mixture should form a
'ball' around the knife blade. If it is still in lumps add
the remaining water but do it gradually. When the
pastry balls up around the knife, stop the processor,
take the blade out of the machine and then the
pastry, give it a couple of pushes with the heel of
your hand to exclude any air bubbles, wrap it in
cling film and chill for 30 minutes.

Crafty Tip

● When using either of these pastries to line a
pastry tin or case that doesn't need a top, you can
save yourself the bother of floured work surfaces
and rolling pins by putting an appropriate amount
into the tin or mould and pressing it out with your
knuckles and finally your thumbs. You can get a
surprisingly even layer doing this and can flatten it
a bit more if you wish with the palm of your hand.
However, as it is going to be filled, no one will ever
know if there is a slight ripple in the bottom, and it
saves an enormous amount of time and bother. This
is something I was taught by that doyenne of
cookery writers from the 1950s, Elizabeth David.

The right glasses

I know it may make me sound like a cheap-skate, but I don't believe it's necessary to spend a lot on a vast array of matching glasses in every imaginable shape and size. Okay, so in the ideal world, red wine glasses are generally larger than white, but beyond that, a single shape will do for all. If you want to extend your range, you could include a sherry/port glass and a sparkling wine flute (see below).

DON'Ts

● Don't choose coloured glass – it totally conceals the colour of the wine.

● Don't buy glasses that are too small – if you already have small wine glasses, use them for port and sherry.

● Never go for the fill-to-the-brim-waisted, schooner–type port and sherry glasses – they're hazardous to handle and do nothing for the wine.

● Abandon saucer-shaped sparkling wine glasses – they kill the bubble and disperse the bouquet. Go for flutes or wine glasses.

● Don't wash wine glasses in dishwashers without salt – it gives them a bloom.

● Never be tempted to fill wine glasses too full. There should always be a good space above the wine where the aroma can collect.

DO's

● Choose a bowl shape as opposed to a cone shape.

● Go for plain, rather than engraved or decorated glass.

● Buy big! Glasses should never be more than half or just over half full, and you don't want to pour too stingy a measure.

● Sherry and port glasses should be scaled-down versions of your wine glass.

● Use tall flute glasses for sparkling wine, or just use your white wine glasses instead.

● Wash up glasses meticulously *on their own* to avoid contamination from other food flavours. Rinse thoroughly to remove all traces of detergent. Drain upside down and polish with a clean tea towel.

● Store glasses the right way up in cupboards to avoid trapping a musty shelf smell in the glass which lingers. If they become dusty, polish before use.

● Always give your wine glasses the sniff test before you pour your wine to make sure they don't smell of anything at all, or it will cloud your appreciation of the wine.

Decanting

Decanters are old-fashioned bits of kit these days. They were originally intended for crusty old red wines and ports bottled with lots of sediment. If you pour wine from a bottle containing sediment, each time you tilt the bottle to pour and right it again, you mix the sediment up with more of the wine which means you have to abandon quite a bit when you near the bottom of the bottle. Very few red wines throw a sediment in the bottle today, vintage ports being the exception. If you intend serving vintage port or crusted port, it is still necessary to decant it to avoid this problem.

To decant a wine with sediment, first make sure the bottle has stood upright undisturbed for at least twenty-four hours before you begin. Then, being prepared to achieve the decanting in one pouring, with a strong light behind the neck of the bottle, pour the wine very gently from the bottle into the decanter, tipping the bottle as little as necessary. As the wine runs very slowly through the neck of the bottle, you can see when the first signs of sediment show and immediately right the bottle, stopping pouring. If poured gently enough, you shouldn't waste more than half a glass

LEFTOVER WINE

If you don't finish the bottle, how long will wine keep? Wine is alive with bacteria, both good and bad. But to work, bacteria need oxygen. In a full bottle with the cork in, there is only a tiny pocket of oxygen available, so bacterial activity is minimal. But in the part-emptied bottle, even with the cork pushed back into the neck, there is plenty of oxygen for the bacteria to use as fuel, and it will work furiously, spoiling the wine in quite a short period of time.

White wine, kept in the fridge, will be acceptable for up to two days, red wine (out of the fridge) possibly for a little longer, although I have to admit that I

cease to find opened wine very pleasurable after only about twenty-four hours. Even wine for cooking needs to be in good order, so should be used up in four days at the most. Gadgets designed to help the fresh storage of opened wine are partially successful, my preferred type being the nitrogen canister (sold in wine shops and by the Wine Society) which you use to squirt a nitrogen blanket on top of the wine, thus excluding oxygen. The gas is inert and so has no effect on the flavour of the wine.

Sherry also has a limited life once the bottle has been opened.

Dry fino and manzanilla sherries are the lightest in style (and alcohol) and keep for the shortest time. Both should be served straight from the fridge and stored in the fridge once opened, where they will remain fresh for up to ten days. Medium or amontillado sherries will keep longer – about three to four weeks – and cream or sweet oloroso sherries should be polished off, once opened, in a couple of months. Decanting sherry is *not* a good thing. It's all right if you plan to serve and finish it immediately, but by storing sherry in a decanter, you will accelerate its decline.

of wine which is left at the bottom of the bottle with the sediment. If you don't trust yourself with this freehand method, you can pour the wine through a filter instead.

Now this is the *traditional* use for decanters, but there are a couple of other occasions when you might still use a decanter or carafe. Firstly, if you are really out to impress, decanting red wine does the trick admirably. Usually you'd save the decanter treatment for smart, expensive wines *but*, here's my tip: you can impress the typical wine snob just as easily by decanting a modest, not to say ordinary, wine. Don't rush out and break the bank, but buy something you like and pour the contents of the bottle into a decanter perhaps an hour before dinner, and lose the bottle. There's no need to declare the wine – if your guests ask, simply put the question back to them. This will make them even more convinced they're in the presence of a great wine – and a super-generous host!

Another time a decanter can be useful is if you find a red wine is tasting very tannic and tough. Oxygen softens the hard edges and enables the wine to capitalise on its potential fruit and personality. Opening the bottle well before it is needed allows only a small surface area of wine to come into contact with the air. If you open the bottle and pour a glass out, there is a larger surface exposed, but this is negligible compared to the effect of pouring the wine through the air into another clean container, such as a decanter. Alternatively, you can pour the wine into a jug and return it to the bottle for serving.

Traditionally all red wines would have been opened well before they were needed to allow them to 'breathe'. Although merely opening the bottle without pouring out a glass allows little room for 'breathing', there's no doubt that old-fashioned wines badly needed a breath of oxygen to soften them up and bring them to life. Now that most red wines are made in a much more approachable style, it's seldom essential to open them up ahead of time. But there are still few that do not improve in the glass, so there's no harm at all in opening red wines thirty minutes or so before serving them, making sure you also pour out a single glass.

The right temperature and how to achieve it

'Ideally white wines should be cool, but by no means numbed into oblivion . . .'

'Wine accessories' are obviously considered to be perfect presents ... And so, unsurprisingly, new gadgets are invented every year. One of these is a wine thermometer, designed to tell you the exact temperature of any bottle of wine. All well and good. But discovering scientifically the precise degree centigrade of any given bottle gets you absolutely no further, as far as I'm concerned, towards knowing when it is perfect to drink. Chilling wine is not a precise science. It depends on all kinds of factors such as the type of wine, your mood, the kind of day. The general rules are sparklers and white wines to be chilled and most reds to be served at 'room temperature'. But how chilled? What exactly *is* room temperature?

Ideally white wines should be cool, but by no means numbed into oblivion (unless the wine is *very* cheap, in which case over chilling is highly recommendable). *All* sparklers should be well chilled; it's positively dangerous to try to open an unchilled sparkling wine, because the cork becomes impossible to control and can fly off. The fridge is a relatively slow way of chilling wine – it can take more than an hour to bring the temperature down satisfactorily. It's quicker to put the bottle in an ice bucket (any bowl will do) containing ice *and cold water*. The water helps speed up the process. Even quicker are the new iced sleeves you can buy, which hug the bottle and force down the temperature very fast. If you need your chilled white wine in a great hurry – buy it ready chilled.

Some red wines – notably juicy-fruity Gamays such as young Beaujolais, young Chianti, other slimline Italian reds and young Loire reds – are refreshing chilled, too. It's even more important *not* to overchill red wine, so go very steady with your chilling technique. A further word of chilling advice: if the wine served to you in a restaurant isn't cool enough, ask for it to be put in an ice bucket; if it's too cool, take it out of any cooling device and leave it standing on the table until you judge it is right – it can go into the ice bucket again if it warms up too much.

'Room temperature' is *not* 'standing next to a radiator' temperature. When the phrase was first coined there was no central heating in existence. 'Room' temperature meant chilly dining room temperature as opposed to *very* chilly cellar temperature. A red wine is automatically at room temperature unless it has been in a cellar or has been otherwise chilled.

2

ENTERTAINING THE FAMILY

While it has its own rewards, cooking for the family is an everyday job, and coming up with new and exciting meals can be something of a challenge. Lack of time is a particular problem with increasing numbers of both parents out at work all day. Here, then, are some fresh ideas for weekday family meals, Sunday lunches, romantic dinners for two and children's party dishes, all of which can be cooked in under forty minutes – even the Sunday lunches!

FIVE 2-COURSE FAMILY MEALS

These meals are designed so that you can entertain effortlessly. They are 'family' in the sense that they are designed for palates of all ages. But they are great to serve to friends and relatives as well as your immediate family. The other good thing about them is that they can be expanded in quantity by doubling up ingredients without significantly increasing the amount of time taken to cook. Each meal is designed to be put on the table in less than forty minutes after you start preparing it. This is great if you are coming in from work and have to entertain or feed the flock at short notice. As always, the meals make use of all kinds of readily available ingredients and are balanced both in terms of flavour and texture but you can mix and match the recipes if you wish.

MENU

Guacamole Avocado Pâté

Plaice Parcels

A light, delicate meal which is suitable for a summer lunch or one of those occasions where flavour matters more than bulk and calories. Look for a really ripe avocado when you're making this dish – it should give slightly at the pointed end without bouncing back. If you are buying avocados to make this dish, or indeed eat in any other way, and you can't find ripe ones, the best way to ripen them is in a brown paper bag in a drawer where they ripen gently without going squashy or bitter. Or, soften in the microwave by heating the whole fruit on High for 1 minute. Buy a jar of Mexican salsa, now readily available, for the perfect accompaniment.

Plaice is one of our undervalued fish. It is regarded as a poor relation to Dover and lemon sole but it is, in fact, a delicate and delicious fish in its own right. With more and more fresh fish counters appearing in supermarkets (as fishmongers themselves vanish from the High Street) you can now get plaice filleted straight off the bone.

Plaice Parcels (see page 32)

Guacamole Avocado Pâté ⓥ

SERVES 4 AS A STARTER

1 small red and 1 small green pepper
100 g/4 oz tomatoes
2 spring onions, trimmed
juice of 1 lemon
½ tsp salt
1 tbsp sunflower oil
1 large ripe avocado
tortilla chips, warmed pitta bread or
    fingers of wholemeal toast, and a bowl
    of Mexican salsa, to serve

Take the core and seeds out of the peppers, cut
into quarters and grill skin side up until the skins are
blackened and blistered. Carefully remove from the
heat, place in a plastic bag and hold it closed for
30 seconds. The skins will then rub off easily. Cut
into small dice. Halve the tomatoes, remove the
juice and seeds and cut the flesh into small dice.
Trim and dice the spring onions, using both the
green and white parts. Mix them together with the
lemon juice and the salt and oil. Cut the avocado in
half and twist out the stone. Scoop out the flesh,
put it into a bowl and mash with a stainless steel
fork until a fairly smooth purée. Stir in the other
vegetables and mix together. If the mixture is a little
stiff, loosen it with a tablespoon of water but check
for seasoning again. Serve with tortilla chips, pitta
bread or wholemeal toast and the salsa.

Crafty Tips

● *The Guacamole Avocado Pâté can be made 2
hours in advance. To prevent it going brown, sit the
avocado stone in the pâté, cover tightly with
clingfilm and chill.*

● You can prepare the *Plaice Parcels*, ready to go
into the oven, up to 2 hours in advance.

Plaice Parcels

SERVES 4

4 medium-sized plaice fillets, about
    100 g/4 oz each
120 ml/4 fl oz Hollandaise Sauce
    (see recipe page 22)
150 ml/¼ pint soured cream, defrosted
    if frozen
100 g/4 oz cooked peeled prawns, defrosted
    if frozen
8 cocktail sticks
2 tbsp fresh snipped chives
seasoning
mashed potato or rice, green beans and lemon
    wedges, to serve

Preheat the oven to 180C/350F/Gas 4/160C fan
(bottom of the Aga roasting oven). Cut each plaice
fillet in half lengthwise. Mix together the hollandaise
sauce and soured cream and add half the mixture
to the prawns and stir. Use this mixture to stuff the
plaice fillets by placing about 1½ tablespoons on
the thick end of the fillet and rolling it up so that you
have a tube of plaice with the stuffing in the middle.
Secure this with a cocktail stick and do the same
for the remaining seven fillets. Stand these upright
on their cut sides in a baking dish into which they
will all just fit comfortably and season well. Spoon
over the remaining hollandaise and soured cream
mixture and bake for 15–20 minutes until the plaice
is just cooked through. Transfer the plaice fillets to
warmed serving plates and remove the cocktail
sticks. Add the chives to the remaining hollandaise
sauce and soured cream mixture and cook gently
on the hob for 1–2 minutes, whisking continuously
until smooth. Pour over the fillets and serve with
mashed potato or rice, green beans and lemon
wedges.

MENU

Pasta Margherita

———

Mini Baked Apples

You can use either fresh or dried pasta for this dish which is a vivid, multi-coloured vegetarian confection with Mediterranean overtones to its flavour. The pudding contrasts the apples' sharpness with a sweet apricot sauce that is easy to make and very attractive to serve.

Pasta Margherita Ⓥ

SERVES 4

350 g/12 oz three colour pasta spirals 🛒
2 tbsp olive oil 🛒 **(see page 15)**
225 g/8 oz mangetout
1 large red pepper
about 6 spring onions
175 g/6 oz Halloumi cheese
   (Middle Eastern cheese now found in
   most major supermarkets)
2 tbsp green pesto sauce 🛒
freshly grated vegetarian Parmesan cheese to
   garnish (optional)
fresh green salad, to serve

If the pasta is fresh, cook it for 4 minutes in plenty of boiling water. Drain, stir in 1 teaspoon olive oil and set aside. If the pasta is dried, cook it for 3–4 minutes in plenty of boiling salted water, then cover with the lid and allow to stand for 7 minutes. Drain, add 1 teaspoon olive oil and set aside. Top and tail the mangetout. Take the seeds and stem out of the red pepper and cut it into 5 mm/¼ in strips. Trim the spring onions, chop the white part and cut the green ends into 5 cm/2 in lengths. Cut the cheese into 5 mm/¼ in strips in the same way as the red peppers. Heat the remaining olive oil in a frying or sauté pan and fry the white part of the spring onions, the red pepper strips and mangetout together briskly for 3–4 minutes. Add 4 tablespoons water and bring to the boil until all the water has evaporated and the vegetables are frying again. Add the cheese, the drained pasta and the green sections from the spring onion and gently stir together for 1–2 minutes to heat the Halloumi through. Add the pesto sauce. If using, sprinkle over a little Parmesan; serve with a fresh green salad.

THREE COLOUR PASTA SPIRALS
Red pasta is coloured with tomato and green with spinach although the flavours are not very pronounced when cooked. The advantage of buying fresh pasta spirals is that they cook in just 3–4 minutes. The dried version, however, can be kept in the storecupboard, sealed, for up to 4 months without any deterioration.

PESTO SAUCE
Pesto sauce is a mixture of olive oil, garlic, fresh basil, nuts and cheese. The cheese can be Pecorino or Parmesan and the nuts, pine nuts or walnuts. You can make your own, but shop-bought varieties are excellent. There are also flavoured versions with tomato and other ingredients added to give them extra zing.

BELOW LEFT

Mini Baked Apples
(see page 36)

BELOW

Pasta Margherita
(see page 33)

Mini Baked Apples

SERVES 4

4 small eating apples, such as Cox's or Russets
25 g/1 oz sultanas
4 tbsp apricot conserve or jam
120 ml/4 fl oz water
pouring cream or custard, to serve

Choose a small baking dish just the size to contain the apples. Preheat the oven to 190C/375F/Gas 5/175C fan (bottom of the Aga roasting oven). Very carefully core the apples leaving a plug in the bottom and gently stuff with the sultanas. Place the apples in the baking dish. Warm the apricot conserve or jam and pour into each apple as much as the space will allow. Let the remainder trickle over the apples. Pour the water round the apples and bake for about 20 minutes or until the apples are cooked through but have not collapsed. To serve, place each apple in a small serving dish and pour over the juices from the pan. Serve warm with cream or custard.

CONSERVES
There are many jams now available with a higher fruit and lower sugar content. These are usually described as conserves and are slightly runnier than old-fashioned jams but with the fruit in larger pieces.

Crafty Tips

● You can prepare all the vegetables and cheese, ready to use, up to 24 hours in advance.

● You can core and stuff the apples the day before so they are ready to bake. Brush the insides with lemon juice to prevent discoloration.

MENU

Light Cream of Tomato Soup

Herby Toad in the Hole with Crisp Tossed Cabbage

This is a quick, crafty meal with the style and flavours of a traditional British lunch. The cabbage technique may not be traditional but I'll guarantee that the results will convert even those people who were put off, for what they thought was life, by the khaki products at school.

Light Cream of Tomato Soup Ⓥ

SERVES 4 AS A STARTER

1 onion, peeled and finely chopped
1 tbsp sunflower oil
1 tsp chopped fresh basil or oregano
   or ½ tsp freeze-dried (see page 53)
700 g /1½ lb jar passata
   (Italian sieved tomatoes)
150 ml/¼ pint chicken or vegetable stock
   or water
1 tsp sugar
½ tsp salt
100 ml/4 fl oz fromage frais (see opposite)

Gently fry the onion in the oil for 4–5 minutes until translucent, then stir in the oregano if you are using it (but not the basil). Add the passata and the stock or water. Add the sugar and salt, bring to the boil and simmer for 10 minutes. Now stir in the basil, if using, and the fromage frais. Do not allow the soup to boil again but serve immediately, piping hot.

FROMAGE FRAIS
This is a French form of low fat cheese which in fact is as much a yoghurt in texture as it is a cheese. The Germans have a version called quark which is drier and firmer, more like a light cottage cheese, which is perhaps best for savoury cooking. The creamier, French-style version is marvellous as a substitute for cream and delicious with pieces of fresh fruit or a good quality fruit conserve stirred into it.

Herby Toad in the Hole

SERVES 4

450 g/1 lb (about 6) beef sausages
1 tbsp sunflower oil
100 g/4 oz plain flour
2 eggs
300 ml/½ pint milk
pinch of salt
2 tbsp chopped fresh parsley
2 tbsp snipped fresh chives or 2 tsp of freeze-dried chives 🛒 (see page 53)
1 tsp chopped fresh thyme or pinch of freeze-dried thyme 🛒 (see page 53)

Preheat the oven to 200C/400F/Gas 6/180C fan (top of the Aga roasting oven). Gently fry the

sausages in the oil for 5–10 minutes until browned all over, then place with the oil in a 39 × 25 cm/ 15 × 10 in roasting tin. Put in the oven for about 5 minutes. Meanwhile, whisk together the flour, eggs, milk, salt and herbs for 2–3 minutes until smooth and thickened. Pour the mixture carefully into the hot pan around the sausages. Return to the oven and bake for about 30 minutes or until risen and golden.

Crisp Tossed Cabbage

SERVES 4

25 g/1 oz butter
2 tbsp water
450 g/1 lb green cabbage, trimmed and cut across the grain into 1 cm/½ in slices
pinch of salt
freshly ground black pepper

Three minutes before you wish to serve, put the butter and the water in a large pan with a tight lid over a high heat. When the butter has melted and the water is boiling, add the cabbage all at once with the salt, place the lid on, shake vigorously and cook over maximum heat for 1½ minutes. Shake again, cook for another 1½ minutes, then remove from the heat. You can drain the cabbage but most of the buttery juices will be coating the leaves. Season with freshly ground black pepper and serve.
Season with freshly ground black pepper and serve.

Crafty Tips

● You can make the soup up to the stage of adding the basil and fromage frais, and trim and cut the cabbage up to 12 hours in advance.

● You can fry the sausages and make the batter 1 hour before cooking.

MENU

Indonesian Chicken Satay

———

Tropical Fruit Salad

Satay sauce is one of those dishes that comes from a specialised cuisine, that of South East Asia, Malaysia and Indonesia. It's a kind of spiced peanut butter so it's not surprising that children love it too. It is, in my experience, the favourite barbecue sauce of all time. In the unlikely event of there being any left over, spread it on toast the next morning for breakfast. It can be as spicy or as mild as you choose. I have suggested a medium level of chilli, but you may want to reduce it.

The *Tropical Fruit Salad* is made possible because of the wide range of exotic fruits now exported to this country. However, don't add too many varieties of fruit as the flavours will cancel each other out.

LIMES
Fresh limes, looking like small, emerald green lemons, are available now throughout the United Kingdom in supermarkets and greengrocers'. They have a wonderful tropical, sharp taste and a juice that's slightly less mouth-puckering than lemons. Limes can be used to replace lemons in most cases and add a slightly more exotic flavour.

Indonesian Chicken Satay

SERVES 4

1 tbsp lime juice
1 tbsp soft brown sugar
2 tbsp soy sauce
4 chicken breast fillets, skinned
225 g/8 oz long-grain rice
850 ml/30 fl oz water
1 tsp salt
1 tsp sunflower oil
6 tbsp crunchy peanut butter
1–2 tsp chilli sauce according to taste

Mix together the lime juice, sugar and soy sauce. Cut the chicken breasts into pieces 2.5 cm/1 in square and about 1 cm/½ in thick and marinate in the lime and soy mixture for at least 10 minutes – up to 12 hours if kept chilled is fine. Place the rice in a pan with 600 ml/1 pint of the cold water. Add the salt and oil, bring to the boil, cover, turn the heat right down and leave for 15 minutes. The rice should absorb all the liquid and be perfectly cooked at the end of that time.

To cook the chicken, pre-heat the grill and thread the pieces of chicken onto bamboo skewers. (These are obtainable in many supermarkets or speciality food shops, especially those dealing with Chinese or Japanese foods. The skewers should be soaked for at least 30 minutes in cold water before use to prevent scorching.) Grill the chicken skewers for about 5 minutes each side. They should be crisp but not dried out. Meanwhile, pour the marinade into a non-stick pan, add the peanut butter, chilli sauce and the remaining water and stir over a medium heat for 2–3 minutes until the whole mixture thickens and blends. The satay sauce will look unprepossessing at first but will turn golden and smooth as it cooks. Heat until it's just bubbling and serve poured over the chicken skewers on a bed of rice.

Tropical Fruit Salad

SERVES 4

225 g/8 oz pineapple cubes, either
   fresh or canned in natural juice
   (an acceptable substitute)
1 mango
2 kiwi fruit
1 papaya
1 tsp angostura bitters

Put the pineapple cubes in a bowl, reserving any pineapple juice. Cut the cheeks off the mango and remove the skin with a vegetable peeler. Cut the flesh into 1 cm/½ in cubes, and cut any remaining flesh off the big central stone and add to the pineapple. Peel the kiwi fruit, cut in half, then into quarters, lengthwise and slice across into 1 cm/½ in pieces. Add to the pineapple. Split the papaya in half and scoop out all the black seeds from the middle. Remove the skin with the vegetable peeler and cut the flesh into 1 cm/½ in dice. Mix together with the other fruit. Blend the angostura bitters into the pineapple juice and pour over the salad. Stir to mix thoroughly and put in the fridge to chill until ready to serve.

TROPICAL FRUIT

Large supermarkets often have a wide range for you to choose from, while ethnic stores and greengrocers are more likely to have seasonal supplies. Buying tropical fruit can be a bit of a minefield so here are some tips to make the process a bit easier.

● Mangoes are ripe if they give gently when you squeeze them lightly in the palm of your hand. The skin should not be wrinkled or spotted with black.

● Kiwi fruit have a long season and should have a little bit of give or they will not be at their best.

● Papaya has an inedible skin which turns from green to yellow as it ripens. If the stalk end of a green papaya has a ring of yellow round it, it will ripen. If not, steer clear. Papaya is also known as pawpaw.

● Pineapple at its best should have an orange-gold skin, firm, fleshy grey-green leaves, and a fragrant pineappley smell. A leaf, pulled from the centre, should come away easily.

ANGOSTURA BITTERS

This tropical ingredient with allspice as the overwhelming flavouring is the substance that gives pink gins their colour. Use it in cooking, to add a slightly spicy flavour to stews and soups, or colour and zing to fruit. Look for the bottles in the supermarket, or local off-licence, with the bright yellow lid and the glass almost concealed by a closely written label. It is very alcoholic so a little bit goes a long way.

Crafty Tips

● You can marinate the chicken and make the fruit salad up to 12 hours in advance.

● The uncooked, marinated chicken is suitable for freezing for up to 3 months.

This is a meal with its roots somewhere in the Greek Islands, where minced lamb is used in a huge variety of ways and potatoes are traditionally cooked with this strong lemony flavour. The pudding is a marvellous combination of flavours with the sweetness coming from honey, used in Greece to flavour pastries and puddings.

Lamburgers and Greek Potatoes

SERVES 4

450 g/1 lb lean minced lamb 🛒
1 tsp freeze-dried thyme 🛒 (see page 53)
1 tsp freeze-dried oregano 🛒 (see page 53)
1 tsp garlic salt
1 tbsp chopped fresh parsley
1 egg
oil, for greasing

For the potatoes:
450 g/1 lb small, new potatoes
2 tbsp olive oil 🛒 (see page 15)
½ tsp salt
grated rind and juice of 1 lemon
Quick Tomato Sauce (see page 19) and
   mixed salad leaves, to serve

Mix together the lamb, thyme, oregano, garlic salt and parsley with the egg and knead for 1 minute to form a close, dense mixture. Divide this into four and shape into hamburger-sized patties, about 1 cm/½ in thick. Heat a lightly oiled, non-stick frying pan and fry the patties, over a medium heat, for 5 minutes on the first side and 7–8 minutes on the other. They will generate a certain amount of fat so

HONEY
Honey comes in 3 main types: runny, solid and blended. Blended honey can be runny or solid but it is a fairly bland product. Look for varieties with the flower of origin on the label e.g. clover, wildflower, etc. Solid honey is runny honey that has oxidized and the taste won't be all that different.

MINCED LAMB
You can find this, fresh and frozen, in butchers' and supermarkets in a variety of grades, and bulk-sized packages. Lamb can be quite fatty, so the best advice is to look for one marked 'lean' or if possible choose the meat and ask the butcher to mince it for you. Minced lamb is, of course, the proper ingredient for shepherd's pie and moussaka.

should not need much extra fat to cook in. They are ready when crispy brown on the outside and still moist on the inside.

Meanwhile, scrub the new potatoes and cut into even-sized pieces, about the size of a walnut. Put the olive oil into the bottom of a pan with a tight fitting lid into which the potatoes will just fit in one layer. Bring to a medium heat, add the potatoes and turn them thoroughly in the oil. Add the salt and the lemon rind, cover the pan and cook over a low–medium heat for 15–20 minutes until the potatoes are only just tender, shaking the pan every now and again. Add the lemon juice, turn up the heat slightly and continue to cook uncovered until the lemon juice has virtually evaporated and the potatoes are tender.

Serve the lamburgers and potatoes with the *Quick Tomato Sauce* and the mixed salad leaves.

ICE-CREAM

You can buy such marvellous commercially-made ice-creams now that it's scarcely worth preparing it yourself, unless you have an ice-cream maker. Look for ice-cream that has a real cream content marked clearly on its ingredients list. Good examples are Häagen Dazs, New England and Ben & Jerry's, which actually has vanilla pods ground up into it leaving little black flecks of intense flavour in the ice-cream.

Honey Cake and Ice-Cream

SERVES 4

120 ml/4 fl oz clear honey 🛒 **and (see page 40)**
120 ml/4 fl oz water
½ tsp ground cinnamon
225 g/8 oz square sponge or Madeira cake
225 g/8 oz vanilla ice-cream 🛒

Put the honey into a non-stick pan, add the water and the cinnamon and simmer for 2–3 minutes over a low heat until smooth, stirring constantly. Cut the cake in half lengthways and then in half crossways into four even-sized pieces and pour the spicy honey syrup over the cake, allowing it to soak in. When ready to eat, arrange the cake on serving plates keeping any surplus syrup to one side. Put spoonfuls of ice cream around the cake and drizzle over any remaining syrup.

Crafty Tips

● You can make the lamburgers up to 24 hours in advance. Simply place on a plate, cover with clingfilm and chill until ready to cook.

● The uncooked lamburgers are suitable for freezing for up to 3 months.

● You can soak the cake in the syrup up to 12 hours in advance.

Jilly's wines for all occasions

Let me boggle you with a few statistics about wine (purely and simply as a means to make everything all the easier, you understand). There are probably as many as 1000 different varieties of wine-making grapes. More than 40 different wine-producing countries export their wines to the UK, where they are widely available in the high street (or the out-of-town megastore). Big wine shops and supermarkets each carry as many as 1200 different wines. We are quite literally spoilt for choice.

BUT although all the figures stack up to indicate there are hundreds of thousands of different wines made throughout the world, it's surprisingly easy to group wines with family resemblances together. Then choices become

GROUP 1:

Inexpensive white with bags of personality
Examples: Languedoc (French) Chardonnay, inexpensive Italian Chardonnay, Languedoc Terret, Australian and New Zealand Riesling and Riesling blends, Chilean or Hungarian Sauvignon Blanc, Argentinian Torrontes, German Morio Muskat, South African Chenin Blanc

Uses:
- For friends when drinking without food
- Pre-lunch or lunchtime wine
- Summer drinking out of doors or on a picnic
- With supper – to accompany virtually anything, except very powerfully-flavoured meats and sweets
- To take to friends or to a party
- As a basis for spritzers, punches and cups

GROUP 2:

Inexpensive red, soft, fruity and easy Drinking
Examples: Oaky Spanish red (Valdepeñas or 'Don' whatever), Romanian Pinot Noir, Australian Shiraz, California Zinfandel, French Corbières, Moldova Merlot, Argentinian Malbec, Italian Rosso Conero

Uses:
- Drinking without food with friends
- Pre-lunch or lunchtime wine
- Summer drinking out of doors or on a picnic
- With supper – to accompany virtually anything, except very delicate fish dishes and sweets
- To take to friends or to a party
- As a basis for mulled wine

GROUP 3:

Celebration Wine
Examples: Fizz to suit your pocket (keep a bottle of crème de cassis or crème de mûre at the ready and you can afford to buy cheaply, simply jazzing up the wine in the glass by first pouring in a few drops of the fruit liqueur). Every wine producing country makes sparkling wine and some of them are, frankly, less than pleasant. Australia, New Zealand, South Africa and California are good – so far they are concentrating on sending us their friendliest wines. The best quality examples declare 'traditional method' on the label. France's best known *appellation contrôlée* fizzes (other than Champagne) are Saumur from the Loire (unreliable); Crémant de Bourgogne made from Chardonnay (often good and good value) and Blanquette de Limoux (unusual grapes – occasionally rewarding

fewer and simpler. Once coralled into groups, it's surprising how distinct one from another the groups are. When picking a wine for a particular occasion, or to go with a precise menu, food and wine writers (myself included) frequently become *very* precise, matching a specific wine to an individual dish (or occasion). But in all truth, it's not absolutely necessary. Where one particular wine may appear ideal, there are loads of other candidates for the job.

Unless you have plenty of storage space in your house the ideal may be to keep a few bottles at the ready to cover you for (almost) any eventuality. Now the way to do this most effectively is to concentrate on the wine *groups* that are most likely to serve your needs, and buy wines from the groups (see below) most relevant to your lifestyle.

wines). Spain's top sparklers call themselves Cava and offer good value at the cheaper end of the scale. Italy is best known for the sweet Asti Spumante, but makes some good dry sparklers from the traditional Champagne grapes Chardonnay and Pinot Noir as well as Prosecco, from grapes of the same name. Germany's Sekts are a very mixed bag and generally not recommendable.

Uses:
To celebrate absolutely anything you care to imagine, without forward planning.

GROUP 4:
Crisp dry white wine – a little bit special
Examples: New Zealand Marlborough Sauvignon Blanc, Loire Menetou Salon, Southern French Viognier, Alsace Pinot Blanc or Pinot Gris, Spanish Rueda or white Rioja

Uses:
- Before a meal, without food, if you're wanting something a little bit special
- To accompany fish and salads at a slightly more formal dinner
- To take to friends on a special occasion

GROUP 5:
Creamier white wine with a fuller figure
Examples: Oaked Chardonnay from almost anywhere in the world, particularly Australia, New Zealand, South African Chardonnay 'sur lie', Australian Semillon or Marsanne, Gewurztraminer, Marqués de Murrietta white Rioja

Uses:
- To serve anytime without food
- To accompany smoked fish, poultry and light meat dishes and swanky vegetarian dishes
- To take to formal parties

GROUP 6:
Classy red with firm backbone but still bursting with fruit and personality
Examples: Oaky Cabernet Sauvignon, particularly from Chile or Australia, California or Chilean Pinot Noir, Chilean Merlot, Spanish oaked Tempranillo or Rioja Reserva, French Fitou, Loire reds such as Chinon and Saumur. Buying French Bordeaux or Burgundy in this category you need advice to avoid spending too much on too unfriendly a wine.

Uses:
- Serve as the mainstay of a dinner party, accompanying all red meat and game dishes

FIVE SUNDAY LUNCHES

Sunday lunch used to be the meal at which the standard roast and two veg was the norm. Today, however, it can be a very different kind of meal. But Sunday remains a time for being with friends and family, one of the rare occasions when people get a chance to sit down and eat together. It's a great time for entertaining. But it is often very hard work for the cook who can be stuck slaving in the kitchen while everyone else reads the papers, goes to the pub or generally amuses themselves. I am not really in favour of all of that, so here are five lunches, two courses each, that can be cooked in under 1 hour. While you congratulate yourself on being cool and relaxed, you should win you plaudits for the results.

MENU

Quick Roast Fillet of Beef with Celeriac Mash

Glazed Individual Apple Pies

This is the crafty version of roast beef and apple pie. It uses an expensive cut of beef so it is not something for every Sunday. But it is delicious and can go very well with the traditional accompaniments of horseradish sauce and mustard. The mash is a little unusual in that it adds another vegetable to the potatoes. This not only tastes good but has the added advantage of reducing the calories in the potatoes as well, so that even those people watching their waistlines can enjoy it.

The individual apple pies make good use of a widely available, ready-baked range of tart bases.

Glazed Individual Apple Pies (see page 46)

Quick Roast Fillet of Beef with Celeriac Mash

SERVES 4

2 tbsp olive oil 🛒 (see page 15)
1 × 900 g/2 lb piece fillet of beef
seasoning
900 g/2 lb boiling potatoes
225 g/8 oz celeriac
120 ml/4 fl oz milk
½ tsp freshly grated nutmeg
salt
25 g/1 oz butter
cooked baby carrots, and mustard or
    horseradish sauce, to serve

Preheat the oven to 220C/450F/Gas 8/200C fan (top of the Aga roasting oven). Take a small frying pan which the piece of beef will just fit and heat until very hot. Add the olive oil and then brown the beef in it thoroughly for 2 to 3 minutes on each side. Remove and place on a baking dish or tray, season generously, put in the oven and leave to roast for 20 minutes. Peel the potatoes and the celeriac, cut into chunks, then boil in salted water for 15–18 minutes until both are tender. Drain and set aside for a couple of minutes. Heat the milk and add the nutmeg and a little salt. Mash the celeriac and potatoes together by whatever method you normally use and add the hot milk. Beat with a wooden spoon until the milk is fully incorporated into the potato and the mixture is smooth. You can add the butter now as well if you wish. To serve, take the beef out of the oven and allow to stand for 5 minutes before slicing across the grain in 5 mm/ ¼ in slices. Serve each person with at least 2 slices on a warmed serving plate with the celeriac and potato purée and baby carrots, and the mustard or horseradish sauce. This is not a roast beef for gravy – use the juices of the fillet when you carve it to sauce the slices lightly.

Glazed Individual Apple Pies

SERVES 4

1 large English eating apple
25 g/1 oz butter
4 × 7.5 cm/3 in butter dessert pastry bases
4 tbsp apricot conserve 🛒 (see page 36)
pouring cream or vanilla ice-cream, to
    serve 🛒 (see page 41)

Core the apple and cut into 12 segments like an orange. There is an apple corer device which will do this for you easily and neatly. Heat the butter in a small frying pan and quickly toss the apple pieces in the butter until coated and hot. Arrange 3 in each pastry case in an overlapping wheel and spread with the apricot conserve, 1 tablespoon to each tart. Place on the lower shelf of the oven in which the beef is roasting for the last 10 minutes or so of the heat being on. Remove and let them cool slightly while you are eating the main course before serving with cream or ice-cream.

Crafty Tips

● Melt the apricot conserve. This makes it much easier to spread evenly over the apples. You can do this in a microwave for 1 minute on High.

● The celeriac mash can be made up to 24 hours in advance. Simply cover with clingfilm and chill until ready to reheat either in the microwave or by steaming.

● The celeriac mash is suitable for freezing for up to 3 months.

● You can also make the *Glazed Individual Apple Pies* up to 12 hours in advance. Toss the apple wedges in a little lemon juice to prevent any discoloration, then prepare the tarts as given in the recipe and chill until ready to bake.

```
MENU
```

*Grilled Salmon Steaks
with Braised Lettuce*

—

Apricot Pancakes

Grilled Salmon Steaks with Braised Lettuce

SERVES 4

4 × 175–225 g/6–8 oz salmon steaks
seasoning
1 tbsp chopped fresh dill or 1 tsp freeze-
dried 🛒 (see page 53)
50 g/2 oz butter, softened
juice of ½ lemon
lemon wedges, rice or potatoes, to serve

For the lettuce:
4 little gem lettuces
1 bunch (about 6) spring onions, chopped
1 tbsp olive oil 🛒 (see page 15)
25 g/1 oz butter
seasoning
200 ml/8 fl oz water

Farmed salmon is not only very good value but has got rid of the dubious, slightly muddy taste it had in its early days. I'm serving it here with a really unusual vegetable, braised lettuce. This is an English dish from the eighteenth century and its recent revival is due to greater interest in vegetable accompaniments. It makes a perfect foil in both colour and flavour to the rich moist salmon.

The apricot pancakes are also a little unusual. They are an adaptation of a dish made in France with apples, but with apricots it becomes less of a rustic pancake and more of a special event – much too good to save just for Pancake Day.

Put a piece of lightly oiled foil in your grill pan. Season the salmon steaks generously, pre-heat the grill and grill them for 4–5 minutes each side, not too close to the heat. Meanwhile, beat together the dill, butter and lemon juice. When you turn the salmon over, add a teaspoon of the butter mixture to the uncooked side of each salmon steak as it goes under the grill. When they're cooked through, spread the remaining butter over them and allow to melt gently.

Wash the lettuces whole in a bowl of water and shake dry. Split them lengthwise so that the leaves remain attached and trim the base. Heat the oil and butter in a pan into which all the lettuce will go – a large frying pan with a lid is probably ideal – add the lettuce cut side down and cook over a medium heat for 2–3 minutes. Turn over to coat in the juices and turn cut side down again. Add the spring onions, seasoning and the water, cover and cook over a medium heat for another 10 minutes. To serve with the salmon, remove from the pan and sprinkle the onions from the pan over the top. Serve the salmon and lettuce with lemon wedges and rice or new potatoes.

LEFT AND BELOW

Grilled Salmon Steaks
(see page 47)

BELOW LEFT

Braised Lettuce
(see page 47)

LEFT

Apricot Pancakes
(see page 50)

Apricot Pancakes

SERVES 4

175 g/6 oz plain flour
300 ml/½ pint milk
**1 tbsp sunflower oil plus a little extra for
    greasing**
2 eggs
175 g/6 oz ready-to-eat dried apricots
½ tsp almond essence (optional)
**caster sugar and a bowl of soured cream,
    to serve**

Whisk the flour, milk, oil and eggs together and
allow to stand for 5–10 minutes. The consistency
should be that of double cream. Shred the dried
apricots with a sharp knife or scissors and add to
the batter mixture with the almond essence if using.
Allow to stand for another 10 minutes or so. When
ready to eat, stir the batter and put tablespoonfuls
into a large, hot greased frying pan. They will spread
out to about 7.5 cm/3 in across. Turn them over
after 1½–2 minutes and cook for another 1–2
minutes until both sides are pale gold flecked with
brown. Transfer to warmed serving plates and
continue frying in batches until all the batter is used.
It should make 12–14 pancakes. Serve sprinkled
very lightly with caster sugar and a bowl of soured
cream on the side.

Crafty Tips

● The pancake batter can be made up to 12 hours
in advance. Cover and chill until ready to cook.

● The *Apricot Pancakes* are suitable for freezing
for up to 1 month.

MENU

Eggs Florentine

———

Brown Rice Pilau

Vegetarian eating is now so fashionable
that even carnivores are quite happy
to manage a meatless meal every now and
again, particularly when it tastes as
interesting as this one. The lightly cooked
eggs on a spinach base with a cheese sauce
is something that everybody enjoys, even if
they were not members of the Popeye fan
club to start with. The *Brown Rice Pilau* is
very much like a traditional dish from the
Middle East known as *Jewelled Rice Salad*
(see page 148) because of the variation and
vividness of the colours in the mixture.

BROWN BASMATI RICE
You will find this in most major
supermarkets and all speciality food
stores under a number of brand names.
Brown rice doesn't have an exceptionally
high fibre content, although it has more
than white rice, but it does have a
wonderful, distinctly nutty flavour and firm
texture. When cooking it, allow at least 15
minutes longer than for white basmati or
long-grain rice.

Eggs Florentine Ⓥ

SERVES 4 AS A STARTER

4 free-range eggs (size 1)
450 g/1 lb fresh spinach leaves, washed
   thoroughly
150 ml/5 fl oz milk
150 ml/5 fl oz single cream
25 g/1 oz plain flour
25 g/1 oz butter plus extra for greasing
pinch of freshly grated nutmeg
50 g/2 oz freshly grated vegetarian Parmesan
   cheese

Bring a pan of water to the boil and slip the 4 eggs
in their shells into the water. Allow to boil for just 5
minutes, remove and cool under running water, then
carefully remove the shells (be careful not to break
them – the yolks are still soft). Meanwhile, bring a
larger pan of water to the boil with a pinch of salt
in it and add the spinach. Allow to cook for 3 minutes
and drain in a colander, chopping at it with a sharp
knife so that as much water as possible runs out.
Put the milk, cream, flour, butter and nutmeg in a
saucepan and slowly bring to the boil, whisking
continuously. Then simmer for 2–3 minutes,
stirring, until it forms a smooth and glossy sauce.
Stir in half the Parmesan and heat until smooth.
Divide the spinach between 4 × 200 ml/8 fl oz
buttered ramekins and put an egg into a hollow in
the middle of each one. Spoon over the sauce,
sprinkle with the remaining Parmesan and flash
under a preheated grill for not more than 1½–2
minutes, until the Parmesan is melted and the sauce
is just starting to bubble. Serve immediately.

Brown Rice Pilau Ⓥ

SERVES 4

225 g/8 oz Spanish onions
2 garlic cloves
225 g/8 oz carrots
225 g/8 oz courgettes
2 tbsp olive oil
450/1 lb brown basmati rice 🛒 (see opposite),
   rinsed under cold running water
900 ml/1½ pints vegetable stock
seasoning
50 g/2 oz flaked almonds, toasted
25 g/1 oz chopped fresh parsley
bowl of thick Greek yoghurt, to serve

Peel the onions and garlic and chop into dice. Peel
the carrots and trim the courgettes and chop finely.
Heat the oil in a pan big enough to take all the
ingredients. Gently fry the garlic, add the onions
and the carrots and cook for 5 minutes. Add the
drained rice and turn until thoroughly coated. Add
the stock, and season generously. Bring to the boil,
then reduce the heat, cover and cook for 25–30
minutes. Add the chopped courgettes on top of the
rice, which by now should be pretty nearly dry, and
allow to cook for another 5 minutes over a very low
heat.
   To serve: turn the pilau, which should still be just
moist but have no free liquid in it, onto a serving
platter and sprinkle with the almonds and parsley.
A bowl of thick Greek yoghurt goes very nicely at
the side of this.

MENU

*Butterfly Leg of Lamb
with Greek Salad*

———

*Yoghurt with Walnuts
and Honey*

This is a method of having roast leg of lamb in less than 30 minutes. I heard of this technique from a number of different sources, using several different cooking methods, including a barbecue. But it wasn't until I tried it myself that I realised just how effective and scrumptious it could be. It needs a boned leg of lamb. You can either do this yourself (see right) or get a butcher to do it for you, in which case you should give about 24 hours' notice. You can serve it with the traditional vegetables that go with a Sunday roast or, for a lighter meal, try the Greek salad that I suggest. The pudding has a touch of the Middle East about it – a combination of walnut, yoghurt and honey that probably owes more to Anatolia in Turkey than the Greek mainland. It's absolutely delicious.

Butterfly Leg of Lamb

SERVES 4

1 leg of lamb, boned (see below)
1 tbsp olive oil 🛒 (see page 15)
1 tsp chopped fresh or freeze-dried oregano 🛒 (see page 53)
1 tsp chopped fresh or freeze-dried thyme 🛒 (see page 53)
1 tsp chopped fresh or freeze-dried rosemary 🛒 (see page 53)
seasoning

Preheat the oven to 230C/475F/Gas 9/215–220C fan (very top of the Aga roasting oven).

To bone the leg of lamb, put it on a good cutting board and use a sharp, medium-sized knife. You will notice that a bone runs close to the edge of the length of the lamb on one side. Split the leg up that bone and carefully peel the meat back off it on both sides. At the fat end you will find a complex group of little bones which you need to remove as neatly as you can. Continue to peel the meat off the bones until you have opened the leg of lamb up into a shape that vaguely resembles butterfly wings. Trim off any excess fat and tidy up the cutting. The idea is to have a piece of meat approximately 4–5 cm/1½–2 in thick across most of its area with all bones, fat and gristle removed.

Brush the meat, particularly on the cut side, with the olive oil and sprinkle with the oregano, thyme and rosemary. Put the lamb in the oven on a rack so that air can reach all round it and roast it for 15 minutes cut side up. Turn it over and roast another 10 minutes cut side down. Take out and allow to stand for 5 minutes or so in a warm place. You can wrap it in foil at this point if you like your lamb not too pink. It will continue to cook out of the oven. Season it with salt and pepper when it's finished cooking and not before.

FREEZE-DRIED HERBS
Freeze-drying is a new technique for preserving herbs. It captures the herb with a fresher flavour and a much brighter colour than the old-fashioned methods of drying did. With freeze-dried herbs you often need more of them for a dish than traditional dried herbs. They rehydrate very well and are best used in dishes with a little extra liquid added.

Greek Salad

SERVES 4

1 medium-sized cos lettuce
225 g/8 oz cherry tomatoes
2 spring onions
half a cucumber
100 g/4 oz feta cheese 🛒 (see page 114)
25 g/1 oz black olives
3 tbsp olive oil 🛒 (see page 15)
1½ tbsp lemon juice
pinch each of salt and sugar
warmed crusty French or Greek-style bread,
   to serve

Wash and trim the lettuce. Split it lengthwise and then slice across with a sharp knife into 1 cm/½ in ribbons. Put these in a wide, shallow salad bowl. Halve the tomatoes, trim and finely chop the spring onions (both green and white parts), mix with the tomatoes and arrange over the lettuce. Cut the cucumber in half lengthwise, scoop out the soft seeds and cut the two halves into very thin half moon shapes. Sprinkle over the tomato and onion mixture. Cut the feta cheese into 1 cm/½ in cubes and sprinkle together with the olives over the cucumber. Mix together the oil, lemon juice, salt and sugar until thoroughly blended and pour in a thin spiral stream all over the salad. Just before serving, give everything a gentle mix so that the flavours blend.

The combination of softness, crunch, sweet and sour is delicious with the lamb, which should be sliced across the grain in 1 cm/½ in thick slices. The warmed crusty French or Greek-style bread is ideal with this.

Yoghurt with Walnuts and Honey

SERVES 4

450 g/1 lb thick Greek yoghurt
6 tbsp clear honey, preferably Greek hymettus
75 g/3 oz walnut pieces

Stir the yoghurt until smooth and swirl in the clear honey, achieving a slightly marbled effect. Crush two-thirds of the walnut pieces, mix with one-third of the yoghurt and honey mixture and place in the bottom of tall wine glasses. Pour the remaining yoghurt mixture over the top and decorate with the remaining walnut pieces. Put in the fridge to chill for 20 minutes or so. It can be kept for about 4 hours before eating – after that the walnuts start to go soggy.

Crafty Tip

● This whole menu can be prepared up to 4 hours in advance. Prepare each dish and chill the lamb until ready to cook, and the salad and dessert until ready to serve.

MENU

Country Captain

———

Peach Fool

*C*ountry Captain is an extraordinary
name for a dish that was developed in
India by the Anglo-Indian community during
the Raj, particularly in regimental messes
where it was the favourite Sunday lunch
dish. I think of it as a chicken curry that is
eaten with the usual curry accompaniments – poppadoms, plenty of rice, chutney
and perhaps a cucumber raita – grated
cucumber and spring onion chopped into a
bowl of thick yoghurt. The *Peach Fool* that
follows it is another Anglo-Indian
development with the marvellous flavour of
fruit blended with cream and yoghurt to
produce a smooth, golden sweet that is the
perfect balance to the spicy main course. I
like to have a few thin, crisp biscuits to eat
with the dessert.

COCONUT MILK
Coconut milk comes in a variety of forms
but I prefer to use the canned version. You
can also buy it in a compressed form
looking like a large block of soap which,
when melted in a little water, turns into
very good coconut cream. The powdered
kinds are fine for drinks but are a bit bland
for cooking with.

Country Captain

SERVES 4

450 g/1 lb onions
1 garlic clove
2 tbsp sunflower oil
1 tbsp mild curry powder or curry paste
200 ml/8 fl oz water
8 chicken pieces
400 g/14 oz can coconut milk 🛒 or
    225 g/8 oz coconut cream mixed with
    300 ml/½ pint boiling water
225 g/8 oz frozen peas 🛒 (see page 74)
1 tbsp lemon juice
1 tbsp light muscovado sugar
poppadoms, plain boiled rice, chutney and
    cucumber raita, to serve

Peel and thinly slice the onions and the garlic and
fry in the oil over a medium heat until the onions
are translucent. Add the curry powder or paste, stir
thoroughly and fry for another 2 minutes. Add the
water, bring to the boil and allow the water to
evaporate until the onions and spices are frying
again and fragrant. Add the chicken pieces to the
pan, turning thoroughly in the spicy onion mixture.
Add the coconut milk, or coconut cream mixture,
stir well and simmer for 20–30 minutes or until the
chicken is cooked through. Add the frozen peas,
lemon juice and sugar. Stir, bring to the boil and
leave to stand for a couple of minutes before serving
with poppadoms, rice, chutney and cucumber raita.

Country Captain

Peach Fool

SERVES 4

**350 g/12 oz peaches or 400 g/14 oz can
    peach halves in natural juice
100 g/4 oz raspberries
150 ml/5 fl oz double cream
275 g/10 oz thick Greek yoghurt
good pinch of freshly grated nutmeg
2 tsp caster sugar (optional)
thin, sweet crisp biscuits, to serve**

If using fresh peaches, dip them into a pan of boiling water for about 30 seconds, then peel them and remove as much flesh as you can from the stones. Cut into cubes and place in a liquidiser with 2 tablespoons of water. If using canned peaches, drain them, cut them into pieces and put in the liquidiser with a spoonful or so of the juice. Purée the peaches until smooth, then clean out the liquidiser and purée the raspberries until smooth. In a separate bowl, beat the cream until it is thick and stiffened. Add the yoghurt spoonful by spoonful and keep beating. The cream will absorb the yoghurt and remain thick. Stir in the peach purée, nutmeg and caster sugar if using, then swirl in the raspberry purée. Pour into tall wine glasses and chill in the fridge until ready to eat. Serve with the biscuits.

Crafty Tips

● You can make the *Country Captain* up to the stage where the chicken has cooked through up to 24 hours in advance. Cover and chill until ready to serve. Then return to the heat, add the peas, lemon juice and sugar and reheat thoroughly.

● The *Country Captain* is suitable for freezing for up to 3 months.

● The *Peach Fool* can be made up to 12 hours in advance without deterioration.

FOUR ROMANTIC DINNERS

Diner à deux, whether it's for a long established loved one or a new and exciting date, is something many cooks contemplate with despair. Producing a delicious dinner is not always conducive to looking one's relaxed and romantic best. I have a few ideas here that might help in this crucial area of entertaining. Not only are the dinners themselves designed to encourage romance, warmth and even passion (if all the legends about certain foods being an aphrodisiac are to be believed), but they are also easy to achieve. All the meals can be prepared in around 30 minutes, though most of them have opportunities for pre-preparation which makes life much easier.

MENU

Thai Prawn Salad

———

Chicken with Tarragon and Crème Fraîche

———

Iced Pineapple Crush

This light meal with its bright, fresh taste is a *diner à deux* with a slightly exotic feel to it. Although the chicken needs finishing at the last minute, it gives you 10–15 minutes before starting to cook when you need concentrate on nothing but yourself. You can adjust the amount of chilli in the first course but the sweetness of the pineapple pudding cleanses the mouth anyway.

Thai Prawn Salad

SERVES 2 AS A STARTER

175 g/6 oz raw large tiger prawns, heads
  removed 🛒
pinch of salt
squeeze of lemon juice
juice of 1 lime 🛒 (see page 38)
½ tsp crushed lemon grass (from a jar) 🛒
1 tsp sesame oil
1 little gem lettuce
chopped fresh coriander, to garnish (optional)

Simmer the prawns in boiling water with a pinch of salt and a shot of lemon juice for 5 minutes until they go bright pink. Remove the shells. Mix together the lime juice, lemon grass, salt and sesame oil in a non-metallic bowl and marinate the prawns in it for 15–20 minutes. Separate the leaves of the little gem lettuce, wash and pat dry and use to form two lettuce leaf cups. Spoon the prawn mixture on top and garnish with a little coriander.

LEMON GRASS
Fresh lemon grass looks rather like slightly dried out spring onions. But, as with so many exotic herbs these days, it can also be found ready prepared and crushed in jars that you can keep in the fridge. The jar version is much the easiest and cheapest way of using it. It is used extensively in South East Asia to add a pungent citrus flavour to soups and sauces.

PRAWNS
Prawns come in all shapes and sizes, but we have come to regard quite small specimens, about the size of a little finger at most, as standard. In South East Asia, however, serious prawns can be the size of two thumbs put together – what we call tiger prawns. You can find raw ones, in most good fishmongers', large supermarkets or Chinese shops. These can be cooked for longer without going rubbery. Pre-cooked prawns, whether fresh or frozen, need to be cooked for only 1 minute (after defrosting).

Chicken with Tarragon and Crème Fraîche

SERVES 2

1 tbsp sunflower oil
1 tbsp softened butter
2 chicken breast fillets
120 ml/4 fl oz water
seasoning
150 ml/5 fl oz crème fraîche
2 tbsp fresh tarragon leaves
new potatoes or small pasta shapes, to serve

Heat the oil and butter in a pan into which the chicken breasts will just fit. When the butter finishes foaming put the breasts in, skin side down, and gently fry for about 5 minutes. Turn the chicken breasts over and allow to cook for another 2–3 minutes. Add the water and leave to cook over a low heat for about 15–20 minutes until the chicken is cooked through. When ready to serve, remove the chicken breasts from the pan and season the remaining liquid generously. Add the crème fraîche to the pan with the tarragon leaves and bring to the boil, scraping up any bits, until the sauce bubbles and thickens. Pour over the chicken and serve with boiled new potatoes or pasta shapes.

CREME FRAICHE
Used a lot in French cooking, crème fraîche is treated with a culture that gives it a light acidity without making it sour, so it is perfect to use in sauces without fear of curdling. It has a 35% butter fat content which is the same as British whipping cream. I also like to serve it, simply, with fresh fruit, and it has an added advantage over normal cream in that it has a fridge life of up to 4 weeks.

Iced Pineapple Crush

SERVES 2

1 small piece of star anise (Chinese aniseed with very glossy seeds)
100 g/4 oz ice cubes
225 g/8 oz fresh, peeled pineapple chunks (you can buy this ready peeled in its own juice in many supermarkets now)
2 tsp caster sugar (optional)

You need a food processor or liquidiser that can cope with the ice – most modern ones can. Crush the star anise in a mortar or, using the back of a tablespoon, on a piece of paper on a chopping board until it is a fine powder. Put in the food processor or liquidiser with the ice, pineapple and caster sugar, if using. Process or liquidise rapidly until the ice is chopped up and the pineapple mixed through it with the spice. Transfer to attractive tall glasses or tall wine glasses. You can then pop it into the freezer to keep for up to 30 minutes before eating. If you keep it for longer, it will set hard and become a water ice rather than a crush.

Crafty Tips

● The *Thai Prawn Salad* can be made up to 4 hours in advance. Cover and chill until ready to serve.

● The *Iced Pineapple Crush* is suitable for freezing for up to 3 months and then can be broken down again in the food processor or liquidiser by whizzing it for 10 seconds.

Chicken with Tarragon and Crème Fraîche

Thinking and drinking laterally

There are some truly magnificent wines in the world which cost a great deal of money. But there are precious few which don't have a *much* cheaper alternative which will give you as much pleasure as the arm-and-a-leg blueprint – or even occasionally more.

On several occasions at charity functions – and even on the *Food and Drink* Christmas Quiz – we've offered guests two glasses of unidentified wines; one containing a first class 'first growth' claret from a good recent vintage, bought for £50–60, and the other a wine made from the same grape varieties in perhaps Chile or Bulgaria, costing about £5. And of perhaps fifty sippers taking on the challenge of deciding which is the £50 and which is the £5 wine, as many as forty have got them muddled up, judging purely on taste that the inexpensive wine carries the top price.

All this goes to show that much of the conceived value of a bottle of wine rests with the label. My case rests that there are plenty of considerably less expensive wines around which, on taste, will challenge the traditional aristocrats. If you're buying wines for a special event, there's no good reason why you should saddle yourself with more expense than you need to. So here I'm going to steer you in the direction of good, inexpensive alternatives to the most lustrous names that you can call upon any time, any season.

'... much of the conceived value of a bottle of wine rests with the label and what it is called.'

LESS EXPENSIVE ALTERNATIVES: RED WINES

To **CLARET:** The major grapes for red Bordeaux wines or clarets are **Cabernet Sauvignon, Merlot** and **Cabernet Franc,** grapes now planted all over the world making juicier, fruitier alternatives to the complex but often tough originals. **Chile** produces some marvellous oak aged tastealikes at excellent prices (try **Cono Sur** or **Errazuriz**). **California,** too, sometimes a bit pricey, but very 'authentic'. Real bargains are coming out of **Moldova** majoring on **Merlot.**

To **RED BURGUNDY: Pinot Noir,** Burgundy's top red grape, is harder to tame than claret's alternatives. Red **Sancerre,** if you can find it, is lovely light, springy Pinot, as is red **Alsace. Chile** again makes good affordable **Pinot Noirs,** as does **California,** such as **Ravenwood,** and don't overlook **England,** our Pinots are coming on a treat. The cheapest if you're after a bargain are from **Romania. South Africa** makes an unusual Pinot cross, **Pinotage,** inexpensive and excellent. Try also wines made from **St Laurent** grapes in **Austria.**

To BEAUJOLAIS: Beaujolais may not be fantastically expensive, but it's worth finding an alternative because the original is less good than it should be. Some southern **Rhônes** such as **Coteaux de Tricastin** and **Côtes du Luberon** deliver the goods, or look out for the **German Dornfelder**.

To RIOJA: The velvet-smooth Reserva and Gran Reserva Riojas have become rarer and pricier, but if you like that vanilla-rich oakiness, look for mature vintages from **Valdepeñas** in southern **Spain**, sometimes classed as **Reservas** and **Gran Reservas**. Oak-aged **Tempranillo** is what you're after, **Navarra** is another good source and the offbeat **Utiel Requena**, or skipping over the Portuguese border **Arruda** is worth a try.

To CHATEAUNEUF-DU-PAPE: The famous southern Rhône wine has similarities to the often modestly priced **Coteaux de Languedoc** wines; try also mature **Corbières** and **Fitou**.

'... don't become too hung up on the protocol of entertaining.'

LESS EXPENSIVE ALTERNATIVES: WHITE WINES

To CHAMPAGNE: The marginal (for grape-growing) climate in the Champagne region of France means that real Champagne can be disappointing. More reliable sparklers come from sunnier climes, notably **Australia** and **California**. **New Zealand** and **South Africa** make delicate fizz, too. Look for 'traditional method' on the label for the top quality.

To WHITE BURGUNDY: **Chardonnay**, the world's favourite white grape variety, is behind almost all white Burgundy and there are few wine-making areas which don't boast a Chardonnay. **New Zealand**'s can be closest to great Burgundy in style – look out for **Martinborough** and **Neudorf** from **Nelson**.

To SANCERRE: The little darling of expense account dining, this Loire Sauvignon Blanc is rather overpriced now, especially on restaurant wine lists. **Sauvignon Blanc** is grown the world over – much cheaper in most places. For economy look for examples from **Central** and **Eastern Europe, Hungary** particularly. Although often no cheaper, for the ultimate thrill in Sauvignon Blanc, go not to the Loire, but to **Marlborough, New Zealand**; you'll never look back.

To GERMAN RIESLING: Germany's poor reputation for her wines has reflected badly on the aristocratic **Riesling** grape (not to be confused with Rizling incidentally; real Riesling is called either simply Riesling, or Rhine Riesling). But **Australia** and **New Zealand** are giving this fragrant grape new life. Look for the grape on the label, or try anonymous white wine blends from either country which don't declare any grape varieties and you'll find they are often in the flowery Germanic style.

To SAUTERNES: For less expensive, sweet white wines I wouldn't look to France. **Austria** makes excellent-value **Beerenauslese**, and the **New World** is now scoring reliably with '**late harvest**' wines which make great sweet drinking.

TASTE THE DIFFERENCE

Above I have suggested well-priced (in the main!) alternatives to well-known wines. But don't become too hung up on the protocol of entertaining. In my house, because for me the new thrill is the new wine, we seldom buy two bottles the same, but instead serve compatible bottles in sequence. You could, for instance, serve two or three different wines from the same group (see below), or you might have two or three different wines made from the same grape variety. Not only is it interesting to compare the wines, but you learn from it as well. Patterns start to emerge, so that you can see how, for instance, Chablis (white Burgundy made from Chardonnay) compares with a Chardonnay made, say, in Australia. The Burgundy Chardonnay is lean, direct, almost lemony, with slight buttery notes and hints of unripe banana and custard, whereas Chardonnay from Australia, almost always matured for a while in oak, has smoky vanilla, cream and rich notes of tropical fruit. By making the comparison, you can painlessly build on your knowledge.

SUGGESTED WINE GROUPS

Wine tasting is very subjective. On this occasion I am recommending the wines, *you* can supply the adjectives!

Chablis
Australian Chardonnay
Northern Italian Chardonnay
—
German Riesling
Alsace Riesling
Australian or New Zealand Rhine Riesling
—
Red Bergundy (not Macon)
Californian Pinot Noir
Romanian Pinot Noir

Touraine Sauvignon Blanc
New Zealand Marlborough Sauvignon Blanc
Hungarian Sauvignon Blanc
Californian Sauvignon Blanc
—
Red Bordeaux
Chilean Cabernet Sauvignon or Cabernet Merlot
Australian Cabernet Sauvignon

MENU

Courgette Pâté

———

*Mixed Mushroom
Stroganoff*

———

Strawberry Pavlovas

Trim the courgettes and cut into 1 cm/½ in slices. Put the oil and butter into a pan and sauté the courgettes for about 7–8 minutes until cooked through and tender. Peel and finely chop the onion, add to the pan and cook for another 2–3 minutes. Using a slotted spoon put the courgette and onion into a food processor or liquidiser and process until smooth. Using the same pan, scramble the eggs in the remaining juices. Season generously and add to the pâté with the mint sprigs. Process or liquidise again until completely mixed. Pour into individual ramekins or a 450 ml/¾ pint bowl, garnish with the mint sprig and chill in the fridge for at least 2 hours. Spread on hot toast or savoury biscuits, or use as a dip for crudité vegetables.

Vegetarian food is often thought to be very stodgy but this delicious menu is full of light and delicate flavours, just perfect for a romantic evening. Whatever your plans the food won't weigh you down. It can also almost all be prepared quite a long way in advance with the exception of the final touches to the stroganoff. The *Courgette Pâté*, I find, is a firm favourite with even the most carnivorous of people and the *Mushroom Stroganoff* quite filling even without its customary addition of beef.

Courgette Pâté ⓥ

SERVES 2 AS A STARTER

350 g/12 oz courgettes
2 tbsp olive oil 🛒 (see page 15)
25 g/1 oz butter
1 small onion
2 eggs, lightly beaten
seasoning
couple of mint sprigs
mint sprig to garnish
hot toast or savoury biscuits or crudité
    vegetables, to serve

Mixed Mushroom Stroganoff ⓥ

SERVES 2

450 g/1 lb mixed mushrooms (try to include
    some shiitake, chestnut or button
    mushrooms, oyster, morels or ceps) 🛒
    (see page 66)
225 g/8 oz Spanish onions
2 tbsp olive oil 🛒 (see page 15)
1 heaped tbsp tomato purée
150 ml/5 fl oz vegetable stock
2 tsp softened butter
2 tsp plain flour
150 ml/5 fl oz soured cream
seasoning
chopped fresh parsley, to garnish
tagliatelle or plain boiled rice, to serve

Wipe clean and trim the mushrooms but don't peel them. If you have trouble finding ceps or morels you can buy them dried and reconstitute them in a bowl of warm water for about 10 minutes. If you do this, use the water as the vegetable stock in the recipe. Slice the mushrooms into 1 cm/½ in pieces. Peel and cut the onions into 5 mm/¼ in slices. Heat

LEFT
Courgette Pâté
(see page 63)

BELOW LEFT
Strawberry Pavlovas
(see page 66)

BELOW
Mixed Mushroom Stroganoff
(see page 63)

FOOD AND DRINK

the oil in a frying pan and fry the onions until softened and translucent. Add the mushrooms, mix thoroughly, and cook for 2–3 minutes. Add the tomato purée and vegetable stock and bring to the boil, stirring until the whole mixture is heated through. Beat the butter and flour together and add that, piece by piece, to the sauce until it thickens and goes glossy – this should only take 2–3 minutes – and then season to taste. The dish can now be left aside for up to 20 minutes before serving.

When ready to serve, heat again to boiling point, take off the heat and stir in the soured cream.

MUSHROOMS
All supermarkets and a number of the speciality shops now sell an extraordinary variety of mushrooms in addition to the ordinary white 'Paris' ones. There are the dark brown **chestnut** mushrooms, usually organically grown, which have a richer flavour and tighter texture. **Shiitake**, from Japan, are grown on oak logs and have an even stronger flavour and firmer texture than the chestnut. They are quite expensive but very much worth it for special occasions. **Oyster** mushrooms tend to be rather flatter and without the typical bell-shaped cap. They come in white, yellow and pink. The colour makes little difference to the flavour which is mild but quite substantial. **Morel** are a spring variety. The conical cap is cream to buff and has a honeycomb appearance; the stem is creamy white. **Ceps** are very rare to find fresh and are usually sold dried under the name *Porcini*. Simply soak these in a small quantity of boiling water, drain and add to dishes as you would with fresh mushrooms. They do have a very intense flavour so use only a small amount.

Strawberry Pavlovas

SERVES 2

4 tbsp crème fraîche (see page 58)
2 individual sized meringue cases
100 g/4 oz small strawberries
25 g/1 oz caster sugar
2 tbsp water

Beat the crème fraîche until smooth and divide between the two meringue cases. Thinly slice half the strawberries and arrange prettily over the crème fraîche. Put the sugar and the water in a heavy-based pan, bring to the boil and stir until it forms a thick clear syrup – do not allow to caramelise. Dip the remaining strawberries into this syrup and arrange on top of the sliced strawberries in an attractive pattern. Allow to cool for about 15 to 20 minutes before eating. These do not keep for more than about 1 hour once they have been filled.

MERINGUE CASES
As with so many baked goods these days, there is now a wide range of ready-prepared cases made from egg white in shops and bakeries. Look for ones that have been designed to hold a filling rather than swirls which should be used to decorate desserts.

Crafty Tip

● You can prepare the stroganoff up to 12 hours in advance. Cover and chill until ready to reheat thoroughly and serve.

Oyster Tartlets

———

Ginger Duck Breasts with Wild Rice Pilau with Asparagus

———

Banana Romance

Oyster Tartlets

SERVES 2 AS A STARTER

6 fresh or canned smoked oysters
1 tsp lemon juice
1 tablespoon water
2 tsp chopped fresh parsley
1 tbsp finely chopped onion
pinch of chopped fresh thyme
pinch of ground cloves
pinch of ground mace
pinch of ground black pepper
25 g/1 oz butter
1 tsp cornflour
1 egg yolk
2 individual sized pre-baked pastry cases,
    approximately 5–7½ cm/2–3 in across
chopped fresh parsley, to garnish

This is a *diner à deux* for a couple who enjoy the richness of the good things in life, a special occasion meal which combines a range of rich and exotic ingredients to produce sumptuous food. Most fishmongers and fish stalls at supermarkets can organise fresh oysters for you, but if you can't get them, canned smoked oysters are a very acceptable substitute, though slightly stronger flavoured. Any other shellfish, like mussels or clams, would be a reasonable alternative too. The duck breasts can be bought now in any supermarket – look for the Barbary duck particularly which is leaner and has more flavour. For the dessert use under-ripe rather than over-ripe bananas.

Put the oysters, fresh or smoked, into a small saucepan. If they are fresh, add any liquid from the shells you have managed to save. Add the lemon juice and water and simmer very gently for 3–4 minutes. Add the parsley, onion, thyme, spices and pepper, stir well and take off the heat. Add the butter. Mix the cornflour in a little water and stir with the egg yolk into the mixture. Bring gently up to simmer – do not let it boil or it will spoil. Spoon into the two pastry cases, sprinkle with a little more parsley and serve warm.

CARDAMOM
Although one of the most expensive spices, cardamom repays with the fragrant and delicate flavours it gives to your cooking. Buy pods which are pale green and you can then split them open to get the slightly sticky black seeds. Simply rub them in your fingers to separate, or grind them to a fine powder.

Ginger Duck Breasts with Wild Rice Pilau with Asparagus

SERVES 2

2 duck breasts, approximately 175 g/6 oz
    each
1 tsp freshly grated root ginger or crushed
    root ginger (from a jar) 🛒
6 tbsp water
1 piece of stem ginger in syrup plus 1 tbsp of
    the syrup 🛒 (see page 122)
1 tbsp light soy sauce

For the Wild Rice Pilau:
25 g/1 oz butter
100 g/4 oz American easy cook long-grain
    and wild rice mixture 🛒 (see page 105)
300 ml/½ pint water
 2 cardamom pods 🛒 (see page 67), bruised
pinch of salt
1 bunch of asparagus tips or fresh
    asparagus spears
seasoning

In a heavy-based frying pan, fry the duck breasts,
skin side down, for 5 minutes over a medium heat
without adding any other oil. The breasts will
produce a surprising amount of fat which will crisp
the skin brown. Pour most of the fat out of the pan
and discard. Turn the breasts over, add the freshly
grated or crushed ginger and 4 tablespoons of the
water, turn the heat to moderate and cook the
breasts for 12–15 minutes until the water has
evaporated and the breasts are cooked through.
Slice the stem ginger very thinly, mix with the soy
sauce and syrup and add to the pan with the
remaining water to create a small quantity of sauce.
Leave to stand for 2 or 3 minutes off the heat.
Remove the duck breasts and slice across with a
very sharp knife into about 10 or 12 slices. Arrange
these in a fan on each plate, add any meat cooking
juices to the sauce and pour over.

To make the pilau, heat the butter in a medium-
sized pan with a tight-fitting lid. Add the rice and
stir for 2–3 minutes. Add 300 ml/½ pint of water,
the cardamom pods and a pinch of salt and bring
to the boil. Turn down to a low simmer, cover and
leave for 10 minutes. Trim the asparagus so you
only have the top 5–7½ cm/2–3 in of the spears
and add to the pan, placing them on top of the rice
rather than stirring them in. Replace the lid and
allow to cook for approximately 5–7 minutes, until
the rice is fully cooked. The water should be
completely absorbed and the asparagus tips bright
green. Serve the pilau beside the sliced duck
breasts with the asparagus tips on top.

CRUSHED ROOT GINGER
As with so many of the more exotic herbs
and spices, ginger now comes not only
fresh but also ready peeled and crushed.
Available in jars, often under the name
Barts (although many supermarkets now
have it in an own-brand version and there
are a number of other producers) the fresh
ginger has just a little oil and sea salt
added to preserve its lovely flavour and
condition.

*Ginger Duck Breasts with Wild Rice Pilau with
Asparagus*

Banana Romance

SERVES 2

2 large, firm bananas
50 g/2 oz butter
2 tsp light muscovado sugar
pinch of ground allspice
juice of 1 lime 🛒 (see page 38)
50 g/2 oz toasted flaked almonds 🛒
vanilla ice-cream (see page 41), to serve

Peel the bananas and slice on the diagonal. Heat the butter in a large frying pan and add the banana slices, cook for 2–3 minutes, tossing occasionally. Sprinkle with the sugar and allspice and pour the lime juice over. Cook for 1–2 minutes until a light syrup has formed, stirring occasionally. Scatter over the almonds and serve with the ice-cream.

TOASTED FLAKED ALMONDS
You can actually buy ready-toasted, flaked almonds, but I think they are easy to make and the flavour is much better. Simply take fresh flaked almonds and cook them in a dry frying pan for about 45–50 seconds – it's very easy to overcook them so don't walk away from the pan.

Crafty Tip

● It's worth noting that all these dishes, with the exception of the ice-cream, will sit quietly for 10 minutes in a warm place after they're cooked, without any deterioration.

MENU

Hot Avocado with Crab Mousse

—

Seared Fresh Tuna Salad

—

Ice-Cream Montmorency

This is a meal, I think, for warm weather with a wonderful rich South of France salad as its centrepiece. It has a delicate, light starter and a rich, self-indulgent pudding with ice-cream and hot, black cherry sauce. The name 'Montmorency' is supposed to come from the noble French family of the same name, one of the Dukes of which had a passion for black cherries and had them cooked with almost everything. There is even a version of Duck Montmorency. On this occasion, however, it's a sauce that's very easy to make in advance and can be heated through at the last minute. Buy the best quality vanilla ice-cream you can – make sure it's full cream ice-cream. As with all the other *diner à deux* meals the last 10 minutes or so before consumption is your own.

Hot Avocado with Crab Mousse

SERVES 2 AS A STARTER

1 large ripe avocado
100 g/4 oz fresh or canned white crab meat
1 tsp mild French mustard
2 tbsp Béarnaise Sauce 🛒 (and see recipe
  page 22)
pinch of salt
½ tsp chopped fresh parsley
lemon slices, to serve

Preheat the oven to 180C/350F/Gas 4/160C fan (bottom of the Aga roasting oven). Cut the avocado in half. You do need a ripe avocado for this even though it will be cooked. Remove the stone and place the two halves, cut side up, in a baking dish, stabilising them with a little crumpled foil. Mix the crab meat with the mustard, béarnaise sauce, salt and parsley and use to fill the avocado halves, spreading a little over the top of the cut surfaces of the avocado as well. Put in the oven for about 15 minutes. Test with a spoon to make sure that the avocado is hot through and serve with a slice of lemon at the side.

BEARNAISE SAUCE
As well as the home-made Béarnaise Sauce described in a crafty easy-to-make form on page 22, there are a number of ready-to-use versions to be found in supermarkets and speciality shops. By choice look for a French brand. Once opened, the sauce should be refrigerated and used within the expiry date given on the label or lid.

Seared Fresh Tuna Salad

SERVES 2

225 g/8 oz small new potatoes
2 eggs
100 g/4 oz French beans, topped and tailed
225 g/8 oz cherry tomatoes
1 cos or 2 little gem lettuces
olive oil for greasing
225 g/8 oz fresh tuna, cut into thin slices
  about 25 g/1 oz each
3–4 canned anchovy fillets, drained
25 g/1 oz black olives
hot French bread, to serve

For the dressing:
4 tbsp olive oil 🛒 (see page 15)
1 tbsp lemon juice
1 tbsp white wine vinegar 🛒 (see page 16)
pinch of salt
½ tsp sugar

In separate saucepans put the potatoes and eggs to boil gently in salted water – they should be done for approximately the same time, about 10 minutes. Rinse them both in cold water, shell the eggs and cut them into quarters. When the potatoes are cool, cut them in half. Boil the French beans in water for 5–6 minutes until they are bright emerald green, drain and run under cold water. Cut the tomatoes in half, discarding the stalks. Wash and pat dry the lettuce, break it up and place in the centre of a shallow salad bowl. Put the potatoes in a ring round the outside of the lettuce followed by the tomatoes, and then by the beans. Brush the grill pan lightly with a little olive oil and grill the tuna slices for 1–1½ minutes on each side or until just cooked through. Then arrange on the salad in overlapping slices and garnish with a criss-cross of anchovy fillets and the black olives. Put all the dressing ingredients together in a screw topped jar and shake. Pour over the salad and allow to stand for 10 minutes before serving. Hot French bread goes very well with this.

Ice-cream Montmorency

SERVES 2

**175 g/6 oz pitted black cherries in syrup
or 100 g/4 oz fresh black cherries,
poached in 2 tbsp water and 25 g/1 oz
sugar for 5 minutes
juice of half a lemon
2 tsp arrowroot
2 tbsp water
225 g/8 oz high-quality vanilla ice-cream 🛒
(see page 41)**

After poaching the fresh cherries in the sugar syrup, remove the stones (if you have the patience). Either way you should have a generous cupful of cherries in syrup. Stir the lemon juice into them. Blend the arrowroot with the water. Stir into the cherries, pour into a small saucepan and bring to the boil, stirring, until smooth and clear. That is the advantage of arrowroot over cornflour although they both have the same thickening effect. Put spoonfuls or scoops of the ice-cream into pretty glasses and pour over the hot cherry sauce. Serve immediately. You can make the sauce in advance and heat it at the last minute if you choose.

Crafty Tips

● The salad can be prepared up to 4 hours in advance.

● Keep the salad and dressings separately in the fridge until ready to serve.

● The cherry sauce is suitable for freezing for up to 3 months.

SIX CHILDREN'S PARTY DISHES

Children's parties are potentially a re-enactment of *Lord of the Flies*, so you don't want to worry about the food as well as everything else. On the other hand if the food is not right the emotional pressure will increase dramatically. Therefore, getting the balance right is crucial. Here are some easy-to-prepare dishes, including some quite smart and delectable cakes. They are not only easy on your time but also have a tried and tested reputation with children of almost all ages. None of these dishes should take more than 15–20 minutes of your time, plus a little time in the oven or on the stove.

Quick Prawn and Pea Pasta (see page 74)

Quick Prawn and Pea Pasta

SERVES 6–8

If there's one thing that competes seriously with pizzas for young appetites it's pasta. This one is very pretty as well as very quick to make – the brilliant combination of pink, white, blue and green colouring is appealing to the child's eye. You can serve it in a big bowl or in individual portions. It's particularly popular with slightly older children – who will be willing to sit down and eat it at a party.

**450 g/1 lb mini shell or animal pasta
  (the multi-coloured kind)
150 ml/5 fl oz single cream
150 ml/5 fl oz milk
2 tsp cornflour
2 tsp softened butter
225 g/8 oz frozen peas**
**seasoning
225 g/8 oz cooked peeled prawns**
  **(see page 57)
50 g/2 oz freshly grated Parmesan cheese**

Cook the pasta in plenty of boiling, salted water for 4 minutes. Take off the heat, cover and leave for 7 minutes. In a non-stick pan, whisk the cream, milk and cornflour together. Add the butter and bring gently to the boil, whisking until you have a smooth creamy sauce. Add the frozen peas and season with salt and pepper. When ready to serve, add the prawns and bring briefly to the boil, for not more than 1–1½ minutes, to make sure the peas and prawns are heated through. After the pasta has stood for 7 minutes, drain it thoroughly and mix with the cheese sauce. Serve at once with the Parmesan cheese sprinkled over the top.

Barbecued Chicken Wings

SERVES 6–8

Chicken wings are very cheap to buy and once properly trimmed almost as good as drumsticks to eat. They are also a great favourite with children because they are not quite so large and unwieldy.

**4 tbsp tomato ketchup
½ tsp chilli sauce (optional)
1 tsp Worcester or light soy sauce
½ tsp garlic salt**
**½ tsp light muscovado sugar
pinch of chopped fresh or freeze-dried
  tarragon** **(see page 53)
pinch of chopped fresh or freeze-dried
  thyme** **(see page 53)
18 chicken wings**

Place the tomato ketchup, chilli sauce (if using), Worcester or light soy sauce, garlic salt, sugar,

---

FROZEN PEAS

These are a great standby and I always keep a bag in the freezer. No one could say they are the most sophisticated of vegetables but they do make a great soup and can usefully be added to dishes like this pasta sauce. Don't buy the minted versions; they're only fit for a rather unpleasant accompaniment to roast lamb and even then they don't taste very nice.

GARLIC SALT

Although garlic salt is easy enough to make by hand – crushing a clove and some salt with a knife blade – I always have a jar of the ready-made kind in the spice rack. It has a long shelf life and adds the inimitable flavour of garlic without any effort.

tarragon and thyme in a shallow, non-metallic dish and mix well. Trim the chicken wings by removing the thin pointed tip leaving just the elbow and mini drumstick. Put into the marinade, mix well to coat and leave for 15 minutes. Put the grill on a high heat and line the grill pan with foil to both speed cooking and simplify washing up. Remove the chicken wings from the marinade, give them a light shake to discard excess marinade and grill them for 6–7 minutes each side. Make sure they are cooked through. You can, when you turn them, dip them back in any remaining marinade to recoat them. At the end of the cooking time, allow them to stand for just a minute because the coating can be very hot and would burn little fingers.

French Bread Pizzas

SERVES 6–8

Pizza seems to be every child's favourite dish these days. This is a very simple method of providing an almost instantaneous pizza.

3 medium-sized French bread batons about 45 cm/18 in long
1 × 140 g/4¾ oz can (5 tbsp) tomato purée
4 tbsp olive oil (see page 15)
1 × 400 g/14 oz can chopped Italian tomatoes with herbs
1 tsp garlic salt (see opposite)
1 tsp chopped fresh or freeze-dried oregano (see page 53)
**225 g/8 oz Mozzarella or a mixture of Mozzarella and Pecorino cheeses, grated **
50 g/2 oz Cheddar cheese, grated
1 × 50 g/2 oz can anchovy fillets, drained, or a handful of black pitted olives (optional)
seasoning

Preheat the oven to 200C/400F/Gas 6/180C fan (top of the Aga roasting oven). Slice the French bread lengthways, spread each piece thinly with the tomato purée then cut into 5 cm/2 in pieces. Mix the oil with the tomatoes, garlic salt and oregano. Season with a little salt and pepper and spread carefully on the tomato purée, making sure that the covering reaches as close to the edge of the bread as possible. Cover the tomato mixture in turn with the grated cheese, again making sure that the cheese covers as much area as possible. You can add anchovy fillets or black olives at this point. Bake for approximately 15–20 minutes until the cheese has melted and the pizzas are hot through.

Potato Wedges Ⓥ

SERVES 6–8

A marvellous alternative to chips which has the added advantage of being lower in fat.

2 tbsp sunflower oil
3 × 225 g/8 oz baking potatoes
1 tsp coarse sea salt

Preheat the oven to 200C/400F/Gas 6/180C fan (top of the Aga roasting oven). Heat the oil in a large baking tray for 5 minutes. Cut each of the potatoes into eight wedges and rinse under cold running water. Pat dry with kitchen paper and add to the baking tray. Toss until coated and bake for 30–35 minutes, turning halfway through cooking. Sprinkle with the salt and serve hot.

MOZZARELLA
You can buy buffalo milk Mozzarella, which is the classic Italian kind, or the Danish cow's milk version in a round piece. Alternatively, ready prepared packs of grated Mozzarella are available with other cheese mixed in – Pecorino or Cheddar (often called pizza cheese) – to use specifically on pizza.

Chocolate Chip Cake

SERVES 6-8

This is always a favourite, combining the most scrumptious chocolate cake with the benefits of bits of chocolate buried in it. You can buy a variety of chocolate chips these days – the dark bitter ones are my favourite – but children often like milk chocolate better. Surprisingly, the chips don't melt in the cooking but remain solid in the cake.

175 g/6 oz plain flour
1 heaped tbsp cocoa powder
2 heaped tbsp drinking chocolate
1 tsp baking powder
1 tsp bicarbonate of soda
100 g/4 oz caster sugar
2 eggs
150 ml/¼ pint milk
150 ml/¼ pint vegetable oil, plus extra for greasing
100 g/4 oz milk chocolate drops
4 tbsp chocolate butter cream or apricot jam (optional)
icing sugar, to decorate

Preheat the oven to 160C/325F/Gas 3/150C fan (bottom of the Aga roasting oven). Grease and base line two 18 cm/7 in non-stick cake or sponge tins.
    Mix together the flour, cocoa powder, drinking chocolate, baking powder, bicarbonate of soda and sugar. Break the eggs and whisk them together with the milk and vegetable oil and beat into the flour mixture for 2–3 minutes with an electric mixer or wooden spoon until a smooth thick batter is obtained. Sprinkle two-thirds of the chocolate drops into the mixture, stir again and spoon into the tins. Sprinkle the remaining chocolate drops on top. Make sure the surface is smooth and bake for 30–35 minutes until well risen. You can check to make sure they are cooked by pressing the top. If your finger mark springs back out then they are cooked, if not they need another minute or two. Allow to cool a little, turn onto a wire tray and cool

completely. You can ice the cakes if you wish or sandwich them together with chocolate butter cream or apricot jam. If you sandwich them together simply decorate the top with a little icing sugar.

Toffee Popcorn

SERVES 6-8

Home popped corn is incredibly cheap and always popular at a party. This recipe combines it with the flavours of a honey butter caramel.

1 tbsp sunflower oil plus extra for greasing
1 tbsp softened butter
50 g/2 oz popcorn
4 tbsp clear honey
50 g/2 oz butter
pinch of ground cinnamon

Heat the oil and the butter in a pan with a tight-fitting lid until sizzling. Add the popcorn, put the lid on, turn the heat up to maximum and shake until the popping has stopped. This should take no more than 4–5 minutes. Make sure you don't burn the popcorn or the oil and butter. In a separate non-stick pan, gently heat the honey, butter and cinnamon, stirring. Heat for 2–3 minutes until the mixture takes on a golden colouring and starts to smell of toffee. Take off the heat and pour over the popcorn in the first pan, put the lid back on and shake thoroughly to mix. Pour onto a lightly oiled baking sheet, spread out and leave to cool a little and harden. Transfer to a serving bowl.

Crafty Tip

● The *Chocolate Chip Cake*, *French Bread Pizzas* and uncooked *Barbecued Chicken Wings* are all suitable for freezing for up to 1 month.

Chocolate Chip Cake

Special drinks for children

Like their parents, children appreciate being offered something a little out of the ordinary to drink on special occasions. In puritanical households where water is the rule, it's not difficult to add a spot of glamour. But most children find juice and squash commonplace, and their parents possibly find the ubiquitous fizzy drink unacceptable. So what do you do? Invent a special recipe and give it an exotic name.

Making a drink as 'non-sweet' as you can get away with gives it the widest appeal to all age groups. As children grow up, so their tastes become a little more sophisticated, tending towards slightly drier drinks. It's entirely a personal matter when and if you decide to introduce your young to alcohol, but the moment is *not* perhaps a big party when you may

be too busy to monitor quantities. Taking the safe route for teenagers (and the only route for children), I suggest some delectable non-alcoholic concoctions providing plenty of opportunity for a spot of theatre in the glass.

Give a bit of thought to the glass and, crucially, the decorations and you can make even the simplest recipe look quite dazzling. There are a wide variety of cocktail accessories available, from parasols, crazy straws, swizzle sticks to plastic animals that hang over the side of the glass. Cubes of fresh fruit skewered onto a cocktail stick, multi-coloured glacé cherries, or slices of orange and lemon are easy to do.

Ice cubes chinking in a glass add panache. Ice cube trays come in a variety of novelty shapes – hearts, apples, pineapples, Christmas trees are just a few. Try freezing fruit juice in the trays for special ice.

LEFT TO RIGHT (see page 80): *Flamingo Lagoon, Pina Colada, Blue Lagoon, Tropical Sunrise, St Clement's* and *Sunset Fizz.*

Sunset Fizz

SERVES 4

The basis is a purée of fresh strawberries – blend them in a food processor or liquidiser, or pass through a sieve. Make this in larger quantities for a punch.

10 medium strawberries, puréed
250 ml/8 fl oz fresh orange juice 🛒 (see page 21)
traditional lemonade
ice cubes
slices of orange and ice, to decorate

Stir the strawberry purée and orange juice together. Divide between 4 glasses and top up with lemonade. Serve an ice cube in each and decorate.

Pina Colada

SERVES 1

Again, this drink could be made in larger quantities for a punch. It will separate after 15 minutes, but is still delicious (some even say the creamy head improves it). If you wish to use creamed coconut simply dilute a small piece in cold water.

25 ml/1 fl oz coconut milk 🛒 (see page 54)
50 ml/2 fl oz pineapple juice
dry ginger ale
ice cubes
canned pineapple chunks
a few cocktail cherries

Pour the coconut milk, pineapple juice and ginger ale into a tall glass and stir well. Add ice cubes. Decorate with pineapple chunks threaded alternately with cocktail cherries on a cocktail stick.

St Clement's

SERVES 1

Another good concoction for a punch if you prefer to make larger quantities.

150 ml/5 fl oz fresh orange juice 🛒 (see page 21)
150 ml/5 fl oz traditional lemonade
ice cubes
1 slice of orange
1 slice of lemon

Pour the orange juice into a tall glass and add the lemonade. Add ice and decorate with the slices of lemon and orange.

Tropical Sunrise

SERVES 1

I have used grenadine in this drink. It is a bright red sweet syrup made from pomegranates. If you cannot find it, substitute any red fruit syrup.

25 ml/1 fl oz tropical or Caribbean fruit juice
25 ml/1 fl oz fresh orange juice 🛒 (see page 21)
ginger ale
grenadine or red fruit syrup
1 cocktail cherry

Pour the fruit juices into a tall glass. Top up with ginger ale and stir to mix. Slowly drizzle in a little grenadine or red fruit syrup, and watch the sun rise. Decorate with a cherry on a cocktail stick.

Blue Lagoon (with Monster)

SERVES 1

Certainly make several of these at a time, but if you want to keep the monster effect serve the drinks already poured into individual glasses so you can add the decoration. Larger quantities as a punch.

50 ml/2 fl oz pineapple juice
4 drops blue food colouring
soda water
2 green glacé cherries

Pour the pineapple juice into a tall glass, add the food colouring and stir well. Top up with soda water and stick the 2 green glacé cherries onto the rim of the glass like a frog's eyes for the monster.

Flamingo Lagoon

SERVES 1

Two variations on ice-cream sodas, both of which go down extremely well with children.

1 tbsp strawberry jam or sweetened strawberry purée (see Sunset Fizz above)
50–85 ml/2–3 fl oz milk
soda water
1 scoop strawberry ice-cream

In a tall glass mix together the strawberry jam or purée and milk. Top up with soda water and add a scoop of strawberry ice-cream.

For a chocolate version use:
1 tbsp chocolate dessert topping, or drinking chocolate
50–85 ml/2–3 fl oz milk
soda water
1 scoop chocolate ice-cream

Follow the instructions above, simply substituting the strawberry ingredients with the chocolate.

3

ENTERTAINING

FRIENDS

One of the greatest pleasures food can give us is being able to share it with friends. Whether it is a dinner party, brunch or barbecue, entertaining friends is a national pastime.

Here is a range of dinner party menus designed to save on time but not compromise on taste. There are four impromptu menus – Italian, Spanish, Chinese and Middle Eastern – and four slightly more leisured ones. If a cocktail party is more your style, you will find recipes for drinks and canapés or, if you prefer cooking outdoors, relax – the pain-free barbeque is here at last.

RUSH HOME DINNER PARTIES

The phrase 'dinner party' never fails to fill me with a sense of anticipation. Firstly, it will be a party (fun and good times for all); secondly, the centrepiece is great food; thirdly, there will be some formality – an event which people have made a special effort to organise and attend. The only problem is that it means the cook has to make an extra effort, and if you're rushing home from work, or like to relax at the weekend, you can end up in a terrific panic, still pushing your trolley around the supermarket half an hour before your guests are due to arrive. Do not worry – help is at hand.

I have devised four crafty dinner party menus designed to be cooked and ready to eat within about 30 minutes.

CHINESE MENU

Hot Prawn Soup

Beef Stir-Fry with Black Bean Sauce

Broccoli with Oyster Sauce

Quick Toffee Bananas

Much Chinese food has the advantage of being cooked quickly, and with the range of Oriental ingredients in the shops it's very easy to make your own Peking-style feast.

You can use chicken stock cubes for the soup but it's much better to buy the intensely flavoured fresh or frozen chicken stock.

The oyster sauce is a kind of thick soy sauce flavoured with, at its best, real oyster extract. The fish flavour is not strong, more a kind of intense savoury taste which goes perfectly with vegetables.

The dessert is a very crafty and quick version of a famous Peking dish which is deep fried. My version isn't and is therefore not quite so sticky or crunchy but a great deal easier to achieve. It's particularly nice served with vanilla ice-cream.

Hot Prawn Soup (see page 84)

Hot Prawn Soup

SERVES 4 AS A STARTER

1 stalk lemon grass or 2 tsp crushed lemon
   grass (from a jar) 🛒 (see page 57)
2 tsp Laos powder 🛒
2 red chillies, seeded and finely chopped
1.2 litres/2 pints chicken stock
2 tbsp fish sauce 🛒 or dark soy sauce
100 g/4 oz button mushrooms, sliced
275 g/10 oz raw tiger prawns 🛒 (see page
   57), heads removed
juice of 1 lime 🛒 (see page 38) or 1 small
   lemon
2 garlic cloves, sliced
a little sunflower oil
2 tbsp chopped fresh coriander, to garnish

Trim and finely chop the fresh lemon grass, if using,
and add it, or the purée, with the Laos powder and
chillies to the stock. Bring to the boil and simmer
for 15 minutes. Add the fish or soy sauce and
button mushrooms, and cook for another 2–3
minutes. Add the prawns and lime or lemon juice
and simmer for another 2–3 minutes until the
prawns are pink and just cooked through. Remove
from the heat for 1 minute while you fry the garlic
in the oil. Pour the soup into a warmed tureen.
Garnish with the garlic and coriander and serve
at once.

FISH SAUCE
This is a seasoning, added as we use salt,
rather than as a central flavouring
ingredient, although it varies from country
to country in its pungency and fishiness.
You will find it in Chinese or Asian stores
and under the Sharwoods brand in
supermarkets. It looks like light soy sauce.

Beef Stir-fry with Black Bean Sauce

SERVES 4

275 g/10 oz beef steak, sirloin or rump
1 tbsp sunflower oil
1 tsp crushed garlic
1 tsp freshly grated root ginger or crushed
   root ginger (from a jar) 🛒 (see page
   68/122)
1 large onion, peeled and thinly sliced
1 large red sweet pepper, seeded
   and thinly sliced
175 g/6 oz baby sweetcorn, halved
   lengthways
1 × 160 g/5½ oz bottle stir-fry black bean
   sauce
4 spring onions, trimmed and chopped
plain boiled white rice, to serve

Slice the beef very thinly against the grain into
1 cm/½ in slices. Heat the oil in a wok or large
frying pan, add the beef and then the garlic and
ginger. Stir-fry quickly until the beef is lightly
browned. Pull to the side of the pan and add the
onion, pepper and sweetcorn. Stir-fry for another
2–3 minutes until the vegetables are just tender.
Mix the beef and vegetables together, add the black
bean sauce and spring onions, bring to the boil
over a high heat, stirring and tossing together for
1–1½ minutes. Serve at once with the rice and
Broccoli with Oyster Sauce.

LAOS POWDER
Also known as galangal and the 'lesser
ginger' this has a slightly lemony taste and
can be bought in fresh, dried and
powdered forms.

Beef Stir-fry with Black Bean Sauce

FOOD AND DRINK

Broccoli with Oyster Sauce

SERVES 4

450 g/1 lb broccoli, broken into small florets
½ tsp salt
4 tbsp oyster sauce

Steam the broccoli or put it into a pan of boiling water and cook for 3–4 minutes until bright emerald green but still just a little crunchy. Remove from the heat and drain thoroughly. Sprinkle with the salt and spoon over the oyster sauce. Return the pan to the heat and stir-fry until just heated through. Transfer to a serving dish and keep warm for not more than 10 minutes before serving.

Quick Toffee Bananas

SERVES 4

4 large ripe but not soft bananas
1 tbsp fresh lemon juice
1 tsp sesame seeds
50 g/2 oz butter
4 tbsp golden syrup
pinch of ground cinnamon
vanilla ice-cream, to serve (see page 41)

You need a non-stick frying pan for this as otherwise the washing up can be a real burden. Peel the bananas, cut them into 5 cm/2 in slices and toss in the lemon juice. Toast the sesame seeds lightly in the dry frying pan for 1–2 minutes until light brown. Set aside on a saucer. Add the butter to the pan and as soon as it has melted add the golden syrup and cinnamon. Bring the mixture to the boil and stir quickly to combine. Add the banana pieces and allow them to heat in the syrup, turning them quickly so they are completely coated. Do so gently to prevent them breaking up. Turn down the heat and simmer for 4–5 minutes. When the bananas are cooked through, sprinkle over the sesame seeds and toss to coat. Serve on individual plates and add a scoop of ice-cream.

OYSTER SAUCE

Oyster Sauce is available in Chinese shops and many British supermarkets. There are 'oyster sauces' made with artificial flavourings – look for one which list oysters in the ingredients! The flavour is quite mild and not obtrusive.

Crafty Tip

● Prepare the Hot Prawn Soup up to 12 hours in advance to the stage of adding the prawns. Cover and chill, then return to the boil, add the prawns and finish cooking.

This menu has an Italian flavour and makes use of some of the marvellous ingredients now available in Britain. When you are making this meal, start by preparing the *Cappuccino Creams*. In a perfect world they should sit in the fridge for a couple of hours but an hour in the freezer works pretty well, and I'm assuming that it will take you 30 minutes to eat the first two courses!

MELONS
Always try to buy melons when they are really ripe. There are two ways of testing this. The first is to press the end furthest from the stalk and see if it gives gently. If it does, it's ripe. The other way is to smell. If you can smell that distinctive fragrance, the melon is ready to eat. These rules do not apply to water melons.

Bresaola with Melon

SERVES 4 AS A STARTER

1 medium sized ripe melon, such as galia or honeydew 🛒
1 packet (about 8 slices) bresaola 🛒
4 tsp fresh lemon juice
4 tsp olive oil 🛒 (see page 15)
freshly ground black pepper

Cut the melon in half, then cut it into quarters and remove the seeds. Remove the flesh in one piece and cut each quarter into three slices, cutting from the outside to the centre rather like large scale orange segments. Arrange 2 slices of the bresaola on each plate and then add the melon, laying the slices in an attractive shape on the plates and filling in the area not covered with the bresaola. Sprinkle a little of the lemon juice over the melon. Pour a teaspoon of olive oil in a trail over the bresaola and grind a little black pepper on top. Chill for up to 30 minutes before serving.

BRESAOLA
This is raw beef that has been air dried without smoking and is moist and rich in flavour. It is a perfect accompaniment to sweet fruit in the same way that Parma ham is traditionally used. An Italian speciality, it comes in wafer-thin slices.

Crafty Tip

● The *Bresaola with Melon*, and *Cappuccino Creams*, can be made up to 4 hours in advance. Cover and chill until ready to serve.

FOOD AND DRINK

Turkey Scaloppini

SERVES 4

350 g/12 oz fresh green and white tagliatelle
1 tbsp sunflower oil plus a little extra
25 g/1 oz butter
450 g/1lb turkey breast fillets
1 tbsp chopped fresh sage or 1 tsp
   freeze-dried sage 🛒 (see page 53)
120 ml/4 fl oz apple juice
200 ml/7 fl oz double cream
fresh green salad, to serve

Put the tagliatelle into a pan of boiling salted water, add a drop of oil and cook for 5–6 minutes until just tender. Drain and toss in half the butter. Arrange in a large oval serving dish and keep warm.

Cut the turkey breast fillets across the grain at an angle so that you have a number of mini steaks, about 5 × 3 cm/2 × 1½ in. If they are very thick you may want to flatten them slightly under a sheet of greaseproof with the back of a frying pan or a meat mallet. They should be about 5 mm/¼ in thick.

Put the oil and remaining butter into a large frying pan into which all the turkey will go in one turn. Heat until the butter stops sizzling and add the scaloppini. Let them cook for 45–60 seconds. Turn and cook on the other side for a further 1–1½ minutes. They should be light gold on the outside but not cooked to a dryness. Sprinkle with the sage, season generously and add the apple juice, scraping up the bits in the bottom of the pan. Transfer the scaloppini to on top of the tagliatelle with a slotted spoon, arranging them neatly.

Add the double cream to the remaining liquid, stir thoroughly and bring to the boil, simmering for 2–3 minutes while the sauce amalgamates and turns pale gold. Pour over the scaloppini and serve immediately. A green salad can accompany or follow this.

Cappuccino Creams

SERVES 4

2 tsp instant coffee
2 tbsp boiling water
300 ml/½ pint whipping cream
25 g/1 oz caster sugar
200 ml/7 fl oz crème fraîche 🛒 (see page 58)
12 amaretti biscuits 🛒 (see page 214)
75 g/3 oz dark bitter chocolate 🛒

Mix the coffee in a small cup with the boiling water. Pour the whipping cream into a large bowl, add the caster sugar and whip the cream until it is just beginning to hold its shape. Fold in the crème fraîche and coffee mixture. Roughly crush the amaretti biscuits and use half the biscuits to fill the bottom of four stemmed glasses. Grate the chocolate and sprinkle a third of the chocolate over the biscuits. Cover with half of the cream mixture and sprinkle over the remaining biscuits. Sprinkle another third of the chocolate shavings on top and cover with the remaining cream mixture. Decorate with the remaining chocolate shavings and chill in the fridge until ready to serve.

CHOCOLATE
Cooking chocolate should always be dark if possible, and a great measure of quality is the amount of cocoa solids in it. Look for something with a minimum of 50 per cent cocoa solids. Some chocolate, especially own-brands from the more sophisticated supermarkets, are up above the 65 per cent mark and this is the best chocolate available. The higher the proportion of sugar and vegetable fats the less favourable the flavour and texture.

Cappuccino Creams

SPANISH MENU

Spinach and Chick Pea Soup

—

Arroz Con Pollo

—

Apricot Swirls

Spinach and Chick Pea Soup Ⓥ

SERVES 4 AS A STARTER

150 g/5 oz young spinach leaves 🛒
1 onion, peeled and chopped
2 tbsp olive oil 🛒 (see page 15)
1 × 400 g/14 oz can chick peas or
    275 g/10 oz cooked chick peas
750 ml/1¼ pint chicken or vegetable stock
seasoning
pinch of freshly grated nutmeg
garlic croûtons, to serve (optional)

Rinse the spinach in a colander and allow it to drain. In a large pan fry the onion in the olive oil until softened and translucent. Add the chick peas and allow them to heat through. Add the chicken or vegetable stock and bring to the boil. Add the drained spinach and cook for about 2–3 minutes, until bright green in colour. Season generously, and add the nutmeg. Transfer to a food processor or liquidiser and purée thoroughly until the chick peas are completely broken up – you may need to do this in two batches. This may take up to 1 minute. Check the soup for seasoning and serve with croûtons, if you wish.

This meal has a strong influence of the Iberian Peninsula. It's arguable that both the soup and the main course have long histories going back to Arab times; Spain after all was ruled by the Arabs for longer than it's been ruled by the descendants of Ferdinand and Isabella who threw them out in 1492.

The soup has a marvellous bright green colour and a surprisingly hearty texture. The chick peas, which give it an earthy quality, can be cooked from scratch. But it is a lengthy process and I usually buy cans of chick peas.

Literally 'chicken with rice', this main course, a version of paella, is eaten all over Spain and substitutes vegetables for the seafood.

Apricots are a great Spanish favourite, eaten both fresh and in various dried forms. This dish is traditionally made with dried apricots but it works very well with those that are canned in their own juice without any added sugar.

SPINACH
This is one of those vegetables that modern growing and packaging techniques have transformed. In every supermarket, and many greengrocers', you can now find pre-packed young, tender spinach leaves which need nothing more than a rinse before cooking or making into marvellous, crunchy spinach salads. Gone are the days of great coarse stems and grimy leaves.

Arroz Con Pollo

SERVES 4

4 large chicken pieces
4 tbsp olive oil 🛒 (see page 15)
2 garlic cloves, peeled and finely chopped
1 large Spanish onion, peeled and roughly
   chopped
1 red pepper, seeded and chopped
1 green pepper, seeded and chopped
2 bay leaves
225 g/8 oz long grain rice
600 ml/1 pint chicken stock or water
small packet of powdered saffron
225 g/8 oz French beans, topped and tailed
2 large ripe tomatoes, peeled, seeded and
   chopped
2 tbsp chopped fresh parsley
mixed salad, to serve

Cut each piece of chicken in half so that you have
eight pieces altogether. Heat the oil in a large pan
and fry the chicken pieces until sealed on both
sides. Add the garlic and onions and cook for about
10 minutes until the chicken is golden brown. Add
the peppers and bay leaves, turning them in the oil.
Now here's the tricky part. You need twice the
volume of liquid to rice so pour the rice into a
measuring jug or bowl, add to the pan and then add
double the quantity of chicken stock or water (about
600 ml/1 pint). Stir the whole pan of ingredients
together, season well and stir in the powdered
saffron. Bring to the boil, cover and simmer for 10
minutes. Add the beans and tomatoes and simmer
for another 5–10 minutes until the rice is tender
and all the liquid has been absorbed. The dish
should be a beautiful gold dotted with the colours
of the vegetables. Sprinkle with the parsley and
serve at once with salad.

Apricot Swirls

SERVES 4

2 × 400 g/14 oz cans apricot halves in natural
   juice
1 tsp cornflour
200 ml/7 fl oz full cream milk
2 tsp caster sugar
1 egg
½ tsp vanilla essence
toasted flaked almonds 🛒 (see page 70), to
   decorate
ginger or lemon thins, to serve

Put the apricots and a little of their juice into a food
processor or liquidiser and process until smooth.
Cover and set aside. Blend the cornflour with a
tablespoon of the milk and set aside. Whisk
together the remaining milk and the sugar in a non-
stick pan and heat gently until the sugar is
dissolved. Lightly beat the egg in a separate bowl
and pour in the milk and sugar mixture and the
slaked cornflour through a sieve. Whisk together,
return to the heat, add the vanilla essence and bring
to just below the boil. Simmer gently until the
mixture thickens and coats the back of a spoon,
whisking thoroughly. Pour into a cold bowl, put a
piece of clingfilm right down onto the surface and
freeze for 30 minutes. Before serving, stir the vanilla
custard into the apricot purée, to create a marbled
effect, and pour into wine glasses or serving dishes.
Decorate with flaked almonds and serve with ginger
or lemon thins.

Crafty Tips

● The *Spinach and Chick Pea Soup* and the *Apricot
Swirls* can be made up to 12 hours in advance.
Cover and chill until ready to serve, then simply
reheat the soup.

● The *Spinach and Chick Pea Soup* is suitable for
freezing for up to 3 months.

LEFT
Spinach and Chick Pea Soup
(see page 90)

FAR LEFT
Apricot Swirls
(see page 91)

BELOW
Arroz Con Pollo
(see page 91)

MIDDLE EASTERN MENU

Tabbouleh

Imam Bayeldi

Spiced Apple and Raisin Filo

Here is a meal with Middle Eastern flavours. It's vegetarian but no less delicious for that. In fact the name of the dish at the heart of the meal, Imam Bayeldi, means 'the teacher fainted', presumably at the total deliciousness of the dish. To speed things up I suggest you use a jar of ready-made Italian-style tomato, onion and garlic sauce sold under a variety of names, *famiglia sugo* or *sugo casa* being the most familiar ones. If you buy large aubergines for this dish they will need cutting up into thick slices, or you can make it with halved small aubergines. Make a little more than you think you will need, because people do develop a taste for this in about 30 seconds flat. This is also traditionally eaten cold as a first course. Allow it to cool gently after cooking, refrigerate for up to 12 hours and sprinkle generously with lemon juice before serving.

Tabbouleh is a very nutritious and delicious salad which is becoming increasingly fashionable in restaurants. Its basic ingredient is cracked wheat, widely available and sold under the name of bulgar wheat, burghul or pod ghouri, depending

on its source of origin. This salad really does have to be made with fresh mint and parsley. If you have one use the food processor for all the chopping.

Tabbouleh (Cracked Wheat Salad)

SERVES 4

175 g/6 oz fine bulgar wheat
3 tbsp extra-virgin olive oil ⛊ (see page 15)
juice of 1 lemon
1 bunch (about 6) spring onions, trimmed and roughly chopped
225 g/8 oz plum tomatoes, stalks and seeds removed and roughly chopped
½ cucumber, cut in half, seeded and roughly chopped
couple sprigs of mint, roughly chopped
50 g/2 oz chopped fresh parsley
200 g/7 oz feta cheese, crumbled ⛊ (see page 114)
1 small cos lettuce
seasoning
warm Arab, pitta or French bread, to serve

Put the bulgar wheat in a bowl and cover with boiling water. It will absorb much of the water and swell up within 30 minutes. When the bulgar wheat has absorbed most of the water, drain it well and stir in the olive oil and lemon juice and then the chopped spring onions, most of the tomatoes, cucumber, mint, parsley and the feta cheese, seasoning generously with salt and pepper. Unlikely as it seems, the bulgar wheat will absorb some of the flavours of the vegetables so if it seems a bit dry do not worry. Line a bowl with separated leaves of the cos lettuce, spoon the Tabbouleh into the middle and arrange the remaining chopped tomatoes in the centre. Let people help themselves, using the lettuce leaves as spoons, and serve with slices of warm Arab, pitta or French bread.

Imam Bayeldi Ⓥ

SERVES 4

1 kg/2 lb aubergines, trimmed
6 tbsp olive oil 🛒 (see page 15)
500 ml/18 fl oz *famiglia sugo* or *sugo casa* 🛒
   (see page 19)
1 pinch of hot chilli powder
1 pinch of dried thyme
1 tbsp torn fresh basil
2 tsp tomato purée
50 g/2 oz pine nuts 🛒
50 g/2 oz chopped fresh coriander

Preheat the oven to 180C/350F/Gas 4/160C fan
(bottom of the Aga roasting oven). Cut large
aubergines into thick diagonal slices or, if small, cut
across in half. Heat most of the oil in a frying pan
and fry the aubergines briefly on the cut sides. If
you want to reduce your oil intake you can substitute
grilling for this process, brushing the aubergines
with the oil and putting them under the grill until
they are very lightly browned. Put the remaining oil
into a pan, add the *sugo*, chilli powder, thyme, basil
and tomato purée and stir until a smooth sauce is
achieved. Arrange the aubergines in a baking dish,
spread the tomato sauce over them, making sure it
goes over them completely, sprinkle with the pine
nuts and bake in the oven for 20–25 minutes, until
the aubergines and sauce are thoroughly
amalgamated and the pine nuts are golden. Sprinkle
over the chopped coriander and serve.

PINE NUTS 🛒
These are about half the size of a peanut
but significantly more expensive. Normally
they are lightly toasted in a dry pan or on
a baking tray in a medium oven before
using. Be careful though, they burn very
easily.

Spiced Apple and Raisin Filo

SERVES 4

6 sheets filo pastry, thawed if frozen
75 g/3 oz butter, melted
50 g/2 oz fresh white breadcrumbs
100 g/4 oz flaked almonds
1 × 400 g/14 oz can spiced apple and raisin
   fruit filling 🛒
a little icing sugar, for dusting

Preheat the oven to 180C/350F/Gas 4/160C fan
(middle of the Aga roasting oven). Place one sheet
of filo pastry in an 18 cm/7 in square baking tin,
brush with a little melted butter and sprinkle over
half the breadcrumbs. Place a second sheet of
pastry on top, brush with a little more butter and
sprinkle over 25 g/1 oz of the almonds. Spoon half
the fruit filling on top. Repeat the layers once more,
then finish with a double layer of pastry. Brush with
the remaining melted butter and sprinkle the
remaining almonds on top. Lightly score the top
to make a criss-cross pattern and bake for
30 minutes. Dust with the icing sugar and serve
warm or cold.

SPICED APPLE AND RAISIN FILLING
This is a relatively new product that several
supermarkets now sell under their own
brand label. It is a mixture of cooked
apples and raisins with a blend of spices
and a little lemon juice for added zest.

Crafty Tip

● This menu can be prepared up to 12 hours in
advance. You can then reheat the *Imam Bayeldi* and
the *Spiced Apple and Raisin Filo* or remove them
from the fridge 30 minutes before serving.

After dinner drinking

'... liqueurs, brandy and port are gradually drifting out of fashion. But, should they slide off the drinks menu for ever, we'd miss them a lot.'

Fashions in food and drink are as clearly defined as they are in hemlines or car design. There's always the *new* cuisine, the hip wine. Our drinking customs shift dramatically and visibly every few years. But one trend which gathered momentum at least ten years ago and is still powering on is the new consciousness of good health. It's led to a move away from the consumption of too much alcohol. So spirits in the shape of aperitifs have taken a nosedive, and another unfortunate casualty of the new alcohol awareness is the traditional after dinner drink.

Although liqueurs, brandy and port are gradually drifting out of fashion, should they slide off the drinks menu for ever, we'd miss them a lot. But their natural position at the end of the meal has made them very vulnerable. Alcohol-aware diners have already run out of puff by the time the meal is finished, so for the time being it's goodbye to Grand Marnier and all that.

But, in keeping with our new, strait-laced attitudes there *are* delicious drinks, relatively light in alcohol, which can step into the recently vacated shoes of the nectars we used to enjoy. Italian Asti Spumante is an unexpected treat at the end of a rich dinner, being deliciously fresh and cleansingly grapey. Sparkling Asti Spumante or the less precisely defined Moscato Spumante is light in alcohol for fizz at only about 8 per cent. As delicious, but less effervescently sparkling and even lower in alcohol, is Moscato Naturale, like a just-pressed grape juice with a refreshing spritz to it. Many after dinner drinks (brandy excluded) are sweet and the lovely fruity sweetness of these moscato drinks works excellently as a digestif. Pineau des Charentes was originally devised as an aperitif (but they treat port as an aperitif in France, too, so you shouldn't be put off by that). It's made in the Cognac region from high strength young Cognac and fresh white or red grape juice. The spirit is added to the juice at the ratio of one part to two, and it preserves the juice intact, without any alteration from fermentation, bringing it up to the strength of about 16 per cent alcohol (or occasionally slightly stronger). Again it is a marvellously fruity drink, silky sweet but this time with slightly more of a sting of alcohol.

However, good though these alternatives are, it would be dreadful to adopt them and simply wave goodbye to the

other delights with post prandial pedigrees spanning back over centuries. One of my particular favourites (and regrettably one of the most punishing in terms of its alcohol content) is green Chartreuse at a thumping great 55 per cent alcohol. Made in a monastery and dating back nine hundred years, using a medley of exotic natural flavourings, it's a magnificent, unforgettable drink.

There's no way, though, I'd be able to handle it after a dinner well lubricated with wine. So I've devised a system whereby once in a while I arrange an evening light on alcohol for the most part until dinner is finished and then I unleash the contents of the drinks cupboard (made up largely of miniatures) on the assembled company. You can simply go easy on the wine during the early part of dinner by having just one glass, or even a spritzer (dry white wine 50/50 with sparkling water), or serve one of the excellent, low alcohol ciders about (much more successful to my taste than low or no alcohol wine). Or it's a good moment to indulge in the new wave of extremely expensive (for what they are) adult soft drinks such as Aqua Libra – to my taste the dry version knocks spots off the original.

'... use port as the focal point of a whole evening, and plan your food and drink delicately to lead up to the post dinner climax.'

If you are matching soft drinks with food, it's important to take sweetness into account. Most wines are dry or medium dry and because of this partner savoury dishes admirably. Fruit juices on the other hand are by nature usually sweet and make less satisfactory companions. Although it, too, has a sugary element, cranberry juice has a kick to it and a dry finish, which gives it more 'dinner appeal'.

Port is nectar and it would be a tragedy if good ruby, tawny or vintage port were to have only one airing in the year on Christmas day. But the spirit alcohol in fortified wines does make them incompatible with an early morning start and a hectic day at the office if they are preceded by other wines before and during dinner. So the trick again is to use port as the focal point of a whole evening, and plan your food and drink delicately to lead up to the post dinner climax. This works particularly well, for instance, if you are planning a light early supper followed by an evening of games which can be deliciously accompanied by port.

INSTANT GUIDE TO PORT TYPES

Ruby: The youngest, cheapest port consisting of a blend of two- or three-year-old fortified wines from more than one year, bottled young while still ruby-coloured. Although they don't have a lustrous pedigree, they can be delicious, with fiery spirit mellowed by intense plummy fruitiness. Don't pay attention to meaningless terms like 'fine old'. Good names to look for are Fonseca, Cockburn and Smith Woodhouse.

Tawny: Genuine tawnies are ports that have been aged in wood for much longer than rubies, so acquiring an amber, 'tawny' colour. But tawnies sold at the same price as rubies are not really the genuine article. They can simply be less special wines with less colour, or even be rubies with a bit of white port added to lighten them up. At the bottom of the price scale, you're better to go for a ruby.

Aged Tawny: Real tawnies are old enough for their colour to have been acquired naturally through protracted ageing in wood and most declare an age on the bottle, such as ten year old, twenty year old, even forty year old. The age is only an average, since tawny ports seldom come from a single year.

They are gorgeously mellow, nutty ports, soft and gentle as well as being fruity as a fruit cake.

Late Bottled or Late Bottled Vintage: Most ports so described are like rubies which have spent longer maturing in bulk – about four to six years – before being bottled. Originally LBVs were bottled without being filtered, so, like real vintage ports, they would continue to mature once bottled and need decanting before serving. The vast majority are now filtered, though, and lose a lot of personality as a result. It's often better to go for a good, honest, young ruby.

Vintage Character: A marketing man's wine! Designed to sound like a vintage, but instead it's actually simply a ruby with five or so years' ageing in wood under its belt. Again, you're often better off buying a simple ruby.

Crusted or Crusting Port: Blends of ports from more than one year, bottled without being filtered so they continue to develop (like a vintage port) in the bottle. Dark, beefy, concentrated wines, they genuinely offer a cheaper alternative to *bona fide* vintage port.

Vintage Port: The flagship of the whole port industry, although accounting for only about 1 per cent of all ports made. In years when exceptional quality is produced, a vintage is 'declared' and young ports from that year are bottled after spending only two years in wood. The wine then takes at least fifteen years to reach its peak – sometimes even as many as twenty or thirty years. Customarily the wine is sold to the consumer in its infancy, and he then has to keep it for all its maturing years before it is ready to drink. A fairly recent introduction is 'single quinta ports'. These are vintage ports from a single property made in good years which are not considered exceptional enough to be declared officially as a 'vintage' year. Although never as intense or special as a true arm-and-a-leg, full-blown vintage from one of the great houses, they *are* vintage ports and have the advantage of being kept by the port house which made them until they are ready to drink. You'll then find them for sale on ordinary wine-shop shelves (unlike declared vintages). Good names to look out for are Quinta do Bomfim (Grahams) Quinta da Cavadinha (Warre) and Quinta da Vargellas (Taylor).

BARBECUES

Barbecues are an increasingly popular form of entertaining but in our British summers they can sometimes be a high risk enterprise.

I have designed some recipes that can be cooked on a barbecue or, if the weather turns grey and cold, in your grill or oven indoors. All these recipes can be served together or on their own depending on the size of your party. None should take more than 10–15 minutes to prepare, plus cooking time.

Turkish Kebabs

SERVES 4

This dish is known across the whole of the Eastern Mediterranean and right up into Northern India. It is a succulently seasoned mixture of finely minced lamb which is pressed around long flat metal skewers before being grilled. Eat it with warmed pitta bread and a tomato, onion and feta cheese salad.

1 onion
25 g/1 oz chopped fresh parsley
450 g/1 lb lean minced lamb 🛒
   (see page 40)
1 tsp dried oregano
1 tsp ground coriander
½ tsp black pepper
½ tsp ground allspice
½ tsp chilli powder
1 tsp salt
a little sunflower oil, for brushing
4 pitta breads
seasoning
tomato, onion and feta cheese salad, to serve

Peel and finely chop the onion together with the parsley in a food processor. Add the lamb and blend together thoroughly until almost a paste texture. Add the oregano, ground coriander, black pepper, allspice, chilli powder and salt, and blend again until a firm, rather sticky texture – this should take another 10–15 seconds. Take the meat mixture out of the bowl, divide it into four portions and roll these into narrow rectangles about 20 cm/ 8 in long. Thread a long flat metal skewer gently through the middle of each one and gently squeeze the meat onto the skewer. Allow the kebabs to set for about 10 minutes, although they will last comfortably covered in the fridge for up to 12 hours. Brush with a little oil and grill for 5 minutes on each side over a hot barbecue. Place the pitta breads on the barbecue for 1–2 minutes before the end of cooking to warm through.

Tandoori Trout

SERVES 4

Fish is often neglected as a barbecue food but in fact it's ideal – quick to cook and easy to handle. It also benefits particularly well from the slightly smoky flavour a barbecue gives it. Trout is ideal because it is a portion-sized fish and its flesh has a natural succulence that helps it to remain moist while grilling. The flavouring here is similar to that used in Indian restaurants but based on some of the ready-prepared spice mixtures you can buy.

4 × 175 g/6 oz whole trout, cleaned
1 small onion
150 g/5 oz natural yoghurt
2 garlic cloves, peeled and crushed, or 1 tsp crushed garlic from a jar
1 tbsp tandoori mix or paste 🛒 **(see page 102)**
seasoning

To serve:
naan bread
yoghurt raita
green salad

Wash the trout under cold running water and pat dry with kitchen paper. Cut off the heads if you want to and slash each trout diagonally twice on each side using a sharp knife. Finely chop the onion and mix it with the yoghurt, garlic and tandoori mix. Season to taste. Place the trout in a non-metallic dish and use a little of the yoghurt mixture to stuff each cavity. Spoon the remaining mixture over the fish, turn to coat and leave to marinate for between 30 minutes and up to 12 hours. Grill close to the coals, that is about 5 cm/2 in away, for about 8–10 minutes on each side or until the skin is crisp and bubbling and the fish is cooked right through. Serve at once with naan bread, yoghurt raita and salad.

Herbed New Potatoes

SERVES 4

As an alternative to baking potatoes in the barbecue coals this recipe offers a number of advantages: (1) the potatoes can be cooked so that they are ready at the same time as the meat; (2) they are always cooked through when removed from the barbecue, and (3) you don't have to scrabble around getting ash and smoke all over yourself to retrieve them. All in all, unrivalled advantages. Everybody loves them and they are the perfect accompaniment for any of the dishes in this section.

900 g/2 lb baby new potatoes
1 tbsp chopped fresh or 1 tsp freeze-dried parsley 🛒 **(see page 53)**
1 tbsp chopped fresh or 1 tsp freeze-dried chives 🛒 **(see page 53)**
1 tbsp chopped fresh or 1 tsp freeze-dried rosemary 🛒 **(see page 53)**
75 g/3 oz butter
1 tsp coarse sea salt
freshly ground black pepper

Cook the potatoes in a pan of boiling salted water for about 8–10 minutes until almost but not quite cooked through. Drain well and return them to the hot saucepan with the herbs and butter and stir gently together. Cut squares of kitchen foil about 30 cm/12 in across and place 7–8 potatoes in the middle of each. Pour over a little of the butter mixture, fold up the sides and screw gently, not to wrap the potatoes tightly but to leave a little air space. You may, if your foil is flimsy, want to use a double thickness. Put the potato packets onto the barbecue grid (or onto the coals at the edge if there's no space on the grid) 10–15 minutes before you want to eat them. You can cook them immediately or chill them for up to 12 hours first. The heat from the barbecue finishes the cooking and you have buttery, herby flavoured potatoes with just a slight smoky taste from the grill. Serve them in their foil parcels, opened up and seasoned with salt and freshly ground black pepper.

Jerk Chicken

SERVES 4

Jerk chicken is a modern development of a process known throughout tropical countries (English speaking ones that is) as a way of preserving meat. It was used on pork and beef as a salting and seasoning process that kept them from going off in hot weather. Now, however, 'jerking', particularly in Jamaica and other parts of the Caribbean, has become a spicy flavouring process similar in some ways to the 'blackened' mixtures used in Creole cooking. Ideal for barbecues, it is much nicer to eat than the rather strange name suggests.

4 × 175g/6 oz chicken breast fillets, skinned
1 bunch (about 6) spring onions
1 tbsp light muscovado sugar
2 tbsp red wine or cider vinegar 🛒
   (see page 16)
1 tsp salt
2 fresh red chilli peppers or 2 tsp crushed
   chilli (from a jar)
2 sprigs of fresh or 1 tsp freeze-dried thyme 🛒
   (see page 53)
avocado and tomato salad, to serve

Crafty Tips

● You can prepare all the dishes in this section up to 12 hours in advance. Simply cover and chill until you are ready to barbecue.

● The uncooked *Tandoori Trout*, *Turkish Kebabs* and *Jerk Chicken* can all be frozen for up to 3 months.

● To make a crafty yoghurt raita, simply mix together 150 g/5 oz of natural yoghurt, 4 tablespoons diced cucumber and 2 teaspoons ready-made mint sauce. Chill until ready to serve.

Slash each chicken breast twice on the diagonal and place in a non-metallic dish. To make the jerk seasoning, trim and roughly chop the spring onions and place in a food processor or liquidiser with the sugar, vinegar and salt, and blend to a purée. Split the chilli peppers, if using fresh, discard their seeds, roughly chop and add them or the crushed chilli to the food processor or liquidiser. Rub the fresh thyme between your hands over a sheet of kitchen paper and add the leaves or dried thyme to the mixture. If using chilli purée and freeze-dried thyme add them straight to the spring onion mixture. Blend all the ingredients together until you have a fairly smooth purée. Smear the jerk seasoning all over the chicken breasts, cover and leave them to marinate in the fridge for at least 30 minutes. They will not come to any harm for up to 12 hours. Barbecue 7.5–10 cm/3–4 in above the hot coals for about 10 minutes on each side until golden brown – make sure the chicken is cooked all the way through. Jerk chicken is excellent eaten with an avocado and tomato salad.

TANDOORI MIX
This is one of a wide range of pre-mixed, sophisticated curry powders. There are a number of brands with varyingly authentic Indian names. All are pretty good used in moderation – that is, far more sparingly than the instructions suggest. There are also paste versions of tandoori flavourings which are equally usable with the same caution. They give a rather bright red tinge to the food which is not necessarily an indication of the level of chilli.

Tandoori Trout (see page 101)

BRUNCH

Legend has it that brunch was invented at a restaurant called Brennans in New Orleans. I'd like to believe in the tale. Brennans is situated in an old plantation-style house set around a courtyard with a fountain in the middle, and the service has that slow but charming southern style to it. However, I suspect that Brennans was the first to formalise what was already a well-established New Orleans custom of rising late and eating a meal that takes the place of both breakfast and lunch. As it happens, it suits our weekend lifestyles as well, and it's a great and easy way to entertain, especially on a Sunday morning.

At its high point brunch seems to be about eating breakfast food, in lunchtime quantities. Here, though, are four substantial dishes, including a sweet, refreshing fruit-based drink, designed to allow for a lie-in on a Sunday morning.

Eggs Benedict

SERVES 6

Eggs Benedict is one of the great American 'combination' dishes, and sadly it has been trivialised in some areas of the fast food market. But, properly made, it's one of the great brunch dishes of all time and using modern resources it is really very easy to prepare.

3 English muffins 🛒
25 g/1 oz butter
6 slices cooked ox tongue
pinch of salt
1 tsp white wine vinegar 🛒 **(see page 16)**
6 eggs
6 tbsp Hollandaise Sauce
  (see recipe page 22)
chopped fresh parsley, to garnish

Split the muffins and toast them. Butter them lightly and put a slice of tongue on each one, trimming it to fit. In a shallow pan of boiling water, put a pinch of salt and the vinegar. Stir this round and lightly poach the eggs in it, one at a time for 2–3 minutes. Place an egg on each slice of tongue and spoon over a tablespoon of hollandaise sauce. You can, if you like, pour the hollandaise sauce into a heavy-based saucepan and warm it gently before using. Do not let it boil! Sprinkle with a little chopped fresh parsley to garnish and serve immediately. The combination is truly delicious.

ENGLISH MUFFINS
These look like slightly large crumpets. They are sold in supermarkets all over Britain and are always eaten split and toasted. They come in plain, fruit and spiced varieties, but use plain ones for Eggs Benedict.

Wild Rice Salad ⓥ

SERVES 6

This dish is rather like a vegetarian kedgeree that has the freshness and luxury of asparagus to give it an extra lift. The combination of wild and traditional rice gives the whole dish an excitement both in appearance and flavour.

225 g/8 oz American easy cook long-grain and wild rice mixture
pinch of salt
450 g/1 lb (about 1 bunch) fresh asparagus
1 bunch spring onions
50 g/2 oz shelled pecan nuts or walnuts
2 tbsp lemon juice
1 tbsp clear honey
1 tsp chilli sauce
4 tbsp sunflower oil
seasoning

Cook the rice according to the instructions on the packet (usually twice the amount of liquid to rice and about 15–18 minutes' cooking time with a pinch of salt). Drain and allow to cool slightly in a sealed bowl. Trim and clean the asparagus, cutting off any woody bits and then cutting the asparagus spears into 2.5 cm/1 in lengths. Trim the spring onions and cut into 1 cm/½ in lengths. Cut the pecan or walnut halves in half lengthwise. Mix together the dressing ingredients, starting with the lemon juice and honey and adding the chilli sauce, oil and seasoning afterwards, whisking to combine. Bring a small pan of water to the boil, add the asparagus pieces and cook for just 2–3 minutes. Add the spring onions, remove from the boil and drain immediately. Reserve a couple of tablespoons of the water and add to the dressing. Reserving a few pieces of asparagus mix the hot asparagus and spring onions into the warm rice, add the nuts and the dressing and stir and toss thoroughly. Garnish with the reserved asparagus and serve warm (although it's perfectly edible cold).

LONG-GRAIN AND WILD RICE MIXTURE

Easy-cook mixtures of long-grain and wild rice can be bought as both supermarket own-brands and under the names of specialist rice manufacturers like Tilda. Don't try mixing the two kinds of rice yourself because unprepared wild rice takes twice as long as ordinary rice to cook. The mixtures are prepared in such a way that they cook well together and produce a marvellous nutty flavour and attractive, speckled appearance – perfect to use in all manner of dishes.

CHILLI SAUCE

Chilli sauces come in two main varieties – the tabasco kind which is quite thin, the same consistency as Worcester sauce and is bitingly hot. A drop or two is usually sufficient. The second kind comes from South East Asia and is usually thick like tomato sauce and, as well as being hot, often has some sugar and garlic added to make it sweet and spicy.

Spring Onion Potato Cakes Ⓥ

SERVES 6

2 large potatoes
2 large carrots
4 spring onions, trimmed and shredded
vegetable oil, for frying
seasoning
Bramley apple sauce, to serve

Peel and coarsely grate the potatoes and carrots – a food processor will do this very well – and squeeze out all the excess moisture. Place in a bowl, add the spring onions, season and mix well to combine. Heat the oil in a large, heavy-based frying pan. Place a 7.5 cm/3 in metal cutter near the edge of the pan, spoon one sixth of the mixture into the cutter and press down. Gently remove the cutter, leaving the cake in place. Repeat two more times. Cook the cakes over a high heat for 4–5 minutes on each side until crisp and golden. Remove from the pan with a slotted spoon, drain on paper towels and keep warm. Repeat with the remaining potato mixture to make six cakes in all. Serve warm with a little apple sauce.

Raspberry and Banana Smoothie

SERVES 6

A pretty and simple dessert that appeals to children and young people as well as those who pretend to a more sophisticated palate.

4 ripe bananas, peeled and roughly chopped
150 g/5 oz raspberries
300 ml/½ pint fresh squeezed orange juice 🛒
** (see page 21)**
juice of 1 lime 🛒 (see page 38)
275 g/10 oz natural yoghurt
6 twists of lime, to decorate

Place the bananas and raspberries in a food processor or liquidiser with a little of the orange juice and blend until smooth. With the motor still running, gradually add the remaining orange juice, the lime juice and yoghurt. (This recipe should make about 1.2 litres/2 pints of smoothie.) Pour into tall glasses and serve chilled decorated with the lime twists.

Crafty Tip

● You can make the *Wild Rice Salad* and *Raspberry and Banana Smoothie* up to 12 hours in advance. However, you then have to serve the salad cold. Simply arrange in a salad bowl, cover and chill until needed. Pour the smoothie into a large pitcher, cover with plastic film and chill.

Wild Rice Salad (see page 105)

Three bottle bar

Cocktails aren't made at home anymore. No one's going to whisk out a cocktail shaker and run you up a Maiden's Prayer (orange juice, lemon juice, Cointreau and gin, for the record). It would be wholly unthinkable. No, cocktails live on only in two places today: fashionable restaurants and bars and in the minds of word-blocked journalists who write about them for want of anything else to enthral you with.

Go for a drink at a friend's house and you're more likely to be given a glass of beer or wine. All very fine, but a shade on the predictable side. The pendulum has swung so hard away from all the frills of the cocktail that I think it's time to ease it back a notch, away from the stark simplicity of the absolutely straight-poured drink and into something a little more daring, a little more original, though certainly not even a quarter as expensive and labour-intensive as a full blown cocktail.

To this end I propose a very simple 'three bottle bar', from which all manner of delights can easily be conjured for any imaginable occasion.

The three bottles I have in mind are:

'... this trio can make at least a dozen thoroughly different drinks to offer and amaze.'

- Dry white wine

- Medium sherry (with a difference)

- Vodka (with a difference, too)

Using as mixers everyday ingredients you might easily have in your fridge or storecupboard, this trio can make at least a dozen thoroughly different drinks to offer and amaze.

Let's take **white wine** first. The wine itself must be properly dry and preferably lean – which means no oak ageing and no Chardonnay. Something such as a Sauvignon Blanc from France or Central Europe would be fine, or a vin de pays such as vin de pays des Côtes de Gascogne. Whatever you do with it it is better chilled, so keep it at the ready in the fridge (or see page 28 if you find you have to chill it in a hurry because you forgot).

SPRITZER –

white wine with pzazz
Half a glass of dry white wine, topped up with sparkling water. Add ice if you like.

CALM BELLINI –

promiscuously fruity
Half a glass of white wine, topped up with chilled peach nectar.

POOR MAN'S BUCK'S FIZZ –

refreshing and long
A third of a glass of white wine, a third fresh orange juice, a third soda water.

KIR –

perennial classic
A dash of blackcurrant syrup (or crème de cassis) in the glass, topped up with white wine.

PATIO SIPPER –

simplest cool punch

Pour 120 ml/4 fl oz lemon squash and the same measure of orange squash into a saucepan. Add the grated rind of an orange, 3 cloves, 1 stick of cinnamon and a pinch of ground nutmeg. Simmer for 10 minutes, strain into a large jug and cool. Add a bottle of chilled white wine and sparkling water to taste.

Second on our list is **medium sherry** 'with a difference': the 'difference' is hot chillies. Buy an inexpensive amontillado or medium sherry and some *slim* green chillies. Prick three or four chillies several times with a sharp knife and post them into the full sherry bottle. Leave for five days and taste for hotness. If the chillies have already made the sherry good and peppery, remove them (this will require temporarily decanting the contents of the sherry bottle into another spotlessly clean container while you take out the chillies, before returning the sherry to the bottle). If sufficient pepperiness has not yet been achieved, wait for a few more days before tasting the sherry again. If you're good with a needle and thread, you could secure the chillies by the tip before immersing them and pull them gently out with the thread when the sherry is sufficiently peppery.

SIGNORITA –
home-grown Bloody Mary
Essentially, this is a Bloody Mary, using the 'hot' sherry as the vodka, and depending on how hot you have made it, perhaps the Tabasco sauce, too. Use a slug of sherry as the base poured on ice, add a dash of Worcester sauce, a squeeze of lemon juice, a sprinkling of celery salt, a twist of fresh ground black pepper and top up with tomato juice. Stir with a stick of celery, taste and, if necessary, add Tabasco sauce.

VIRGIN SIGNORITA –
all the spice but no alcohol
This is simply spiced tomato juice as in the Signorita – but without the sherry, and with Tabasco sauce added.

MATADOR –
deliciously different
Over ice pour a measure (as you like) of spicy sherry. Top up with beef consommé and season with salt and fresh black pepper. Taste, and add Tabasco sauce if you wish.

Third on our list we have **vodka 'with a difference'**: the 'difference' this time is lemon peel or lime peel. Any vodka will do, and buy also an unwaxed lemon or a couple of limes and give them a good scrub. Remove the peel of either the lemon or the limes, trying to take off as little pith with it as possible. Cut into narrow strips and post your choice of fruit peel through the neck of the full bottle. Leave for a week and in plenty of time before using place the full bottle in the freezer (don't worry, the vodka won't freeze because of the alcohol level). The wonderfully citrusy, ice-cold vodka can then be used as the basis for as many delicious drinks as you care to dream up.

If you want to add a bit of theatre to the bottle, you can freeze it inside a column of cracked glass. Here's how: take a plastic 3 litre/3½ pint soft drink or mineral water bottle and cut it off horizontally below the neck. Place the vodka bottle inside and fill the plastic bottle with water to the shoulders of the vodka bottle. Centre the vodka bottle within it and carefully place upright in your freezer. Once the water has frozen, you can take the contraption out of the freezer and run the plastic bottle under a cold tap until it comes away from the ice. Remove it and the ice cladding will remain attached to the vodka bottle and crackle prettily with exposure to the air. So long as you return the iced bottle to the freezer as soon as you have finished with it each time, the ice cladding will last as long as the vodka.

LEMON VODKA ON THE ROCKS –
straight and cool
I'm afraid that's all there is to it, just pour it over ice and drink it straight. Or if you prefer to dispense with the rocks and use a little glass *à la russe*, the vodka is cold enough from the freezer.

LEMON SCREWDRIVER –
old favourite; new twist
Deliciously refreshing with orange juice, the citrus flavour of the vodka just peps it up.

LEMON VODKA TONIC –
v. and t. . . . plus l
As simple as that.

EAST COASTER –
cool from the USA
To a slug of freezing vodka, add the juice of half a lime and top up with cranberry juice to taste.

LEMON MOSCOW MULE –
easy and chic
To a measure of the vodka add a twist of lime peel, the juice of half a lime and top up with ginger ale or ginger beer.

CANAPES

Preparing canapés can be a pain and if you're not careful they can take hours to make only to be devoured by your insouciant guests in a nano-second. These canapés can be eaten that quickly but tend to attract a little more attention and certainly won't take you more than an hour to make. This allows for 12 people eating a generous 12 canapés per person with some of each variety. Arrange them on large serving platters, mixing and matching the various shapes.

Mini Ratatouille Tarts (V)

MAKES 48

For this recipe you need the ready-prepared little pastry tarts, sometimes known as mini croustades, that can be bought in packs of 24 in major supermarkets and delicatessens. The filling is the same as that used in a ratatouille but cut very fine so that it both cooks and can be eaten without any effort.

**175 g/6 oz small aubergine
175 g/6 oz onions, peeled
175 g/6 oz courgettes
175 g/6 oz red pepper
175 g/6 oz tomatoes
3 tbsp olive oil (see page 15)
2 garlic cloves, peeled and crushed, or 1 tsp
   crushed garlic (from a jar)
2 tbsp sun-dried tomato paste or tomato purée
1 tbsp chopped fresh parsley
50 g/2 oz butter, melted
48 canapé-sized tart shells (mini croustades)
seasoning**

Trim all the vegetables and cut into very small dice. You can do this in a food processor but must be very careful not to produce a purée. Heat the olive oil in a non-stick pan, add the vegetables, garlic and sun-dried tomato paste or tomato purée and cook for 10–15 minutes over a high heat, stirring continuously until they are cooked through and the onion is completely translucent. Season generously, stir in the parsley and leave to cool.

Brush the insides of the pastry shells with a little melted butter and leave to set. Fill each pastry shell with a heaped teaspoon of the ratatouille mixture. Do not fill the pastry shells more than two hours before you wish to eat them or the mixture will make them go soggy. To serve them hot, place in a pre-heated oven at 200C/400F/Gas 6/180C fan (top of the Aga roasting oven), for about 5 minutes or until just heated through. However, they are equally successful cold.

Dates with Garlic Herb Cheese ⓥ

MAKES 24

Now we can buy fresh dates all year round and the ones I have in mind are nearly 5 cm/2 in long and have a lovely, succulent, dry sweetness to them. The combination of garlic and dates, by the way, is traditional in the Middle East and is a surprisingly happy one.

24 (about 450 g/1 lb) fresh dates
100 g/4 oz garlic and herb cheese
100 g/4 oz cottage cheese
1 tbsp snipped fresh or freeze-dried
   chives 🛒 (see page 53)

With a sharp knife cut the dates lengthways along just one side, remove the stones and any remaining stalk. Cream the garlic and herb cheese and cottage cheese together and, using a teaspoon or a piping bag, fill the space where the stones came from, leaving some of the cheese showing at the top of the date. Sprinkle lightly with the snipped chives and serve. These will keep covered and chilled for up to 2 hours.

Asparagus Rolls ⓥ

MAKES 24

You need soft brown bread for this recipe and I would suggest a sliced loaf as the bread is evenly cut and easy to use. It also saves time. These asparagus rolls look pretty and have a marvellous texture.

40 g/1½ oz butter, softened
6 slices soft brown bread, crusts removed
25 g/1 oz walnut pieces, crushed
seasoning
6 thick asparagus spears, cut into
   10 cm/4 in pieces (use canned ones if
   you're in a real rush)

Butter the bread, sprinkle each slice with a little of the crushed walnut and season with a little salt and pepper. If using fresh asparagus cook it in a pan of boiling salted water for 4–5 minutes or until just tender. Drain and leave to cool a little. Lay a drained asparagus spear on one side of the bread and roll up tightly and carefully. There should be enough butter to keep the roll closed up. Roll under the palm for a moment to make sure the whole thing stays together and set aside until you have finished all six. Trim the ends off each roll and cut through vertically into four mini cartwheels and arrange on a serving plate.

Prawn and Dill Barquettes

MAKES 24

This classic combination of prawns, mayonnaise and dill makes a succulent and pretty filling for the boat-shaped canapé cases called barquettes.

24 barquettes or frozen cocktail sized
   vol-au-vent cases
a little beaten egg (if using vol-au-vent cases)
1 tsp fresh lemon juice
175 g/6 oz Mayonnaise (see recipe page 15)
3 tbsp very finely chopped fresh dill
350 g/12 oz peeled cooked prawns, defrosted
   if frozen 🛒 (see page 57)

Preheat the oven to 220C/425F/Gas 7 (top of the Aga roasting oven), if using the vol-au-vent cases. Place the frozen cases on a baking sheet 1 cm/½ in apart and carefully glaze the rim only with beaten egg. Place in the top half of the oven, after 8 minutes turn around and bake for another 5–7 minutes until golden brown. Cool on a wire tray, pull out the lids and discard any soggy pastry.

Mix the lemon juice into the mayonnaise with the chopped dill. Make sure the prawns are thoroughly defrosted and drained if frozen, and stir into the mayonnaise mixture. Use to fill barquette or vol-au-vent cases. Don't fill for more than 30 minutes before you are ready to serve or they will go soggy.

Feta and Tomato Kebabs

MAKES 12

This kebab recipe has a lovely Mediterranean flavour and appearance. Buy the smallest cherry tomatoes you can find. Not only is this more economic, it looks better too. You may wish to stick 3 or 4 kebabs into half a lemon as a means of serving them attractively. You can use short bamboo skewers or, if you can't get hold of them, cocktail sticks.

225 g/8 oz feta cheese, cut into
    24 × 1 cm/½ in cubes
350 g/12 oz (about 24) cherry tomatoes
2 tbsp extra virgin olive oil (see page 15)
1 tsp fresh or freeze-dried oregano (see page 53)
juice of half a lemon

Thread a cube of feta, a tomato, a cube of feta and another tomato onto small bamboo skewers or cocktail sticks. Place in a flat dish. Mix together the olive oil, oregano and lemon juice and pour over the kebabs. Marinate for 15 minutes or up to 2 hours. Transfer to a serving plate and serve chilled.

FETA CHEESE
This is a very white, salty cheese originally from Turkey and Greece where it was made using sheep's milk. Now it is often manufactured from cows' milk in Denmark or Germany. You can buy it in large blocks, usually wrapped in plastic to keep it moist, or cut in cubes in bottles of seasoned oil. The latter is an excellent piece of advance preparation for *Feta and Tomato Kebabs*.

Mini Chicken Tikka

MAKES 12

In an ideal world these make excellent hot canapés, although they're perfectly delicious eaten cold as well. Once again you can use cocktail sticks for the bamboo skewers.

350 g/12 oz chicken breast fillets, skinned
3 tbsp natural yoghurt
2 garlic cloves, peeled and crushed, or 1 tsp crushed garlic (from a jar)
1 tsp crushed ginger (from a jar) (see page 68)
pinch of salt
2 tsp tandoori mix (see page 102)
2 tbsp mango chutney (either the smooth version or with finely chopped pieces of mango)
shredded lettuce, to serve

Cut the chicken into 1 cm/½ in cubes. Mix together the yoghurt, garlic, ginger, salt and tandoori mix and stir in the chicken cubes. Leave to marinate for at least 30 minutes or up to 12 hours. Arrange on bamboo skewers or cocktail sticks, about three cubes to a skewer, and grill for 2–3 minutes on each side. Pack them fairly tightly together when you do this so that the heat is evenly spread. When they are cooked, i.e. browned but not baked hard, brush with a little mango chutney and serve hot, or allow to cool and chill them for up to 2 hours. A bed of shredded lettuce is the most attractive way of presenting them.

Crafty Tip

● All of these canapés, with the exception of the *Prawn and Dill Barquettes*, can be made up to 2 hours in advance. Simply arrange on serving plates, cover with clingfilm and chill until needed.

THE CRAFTY LEISURED DINNER PARTY

On occasions there is a little extra time to spend both on the cooking and on yourself and this is the opportunity for the more leisured dinner party. However, even these are still meant to be crafty and are pretty quick to assemble. There's no point in using up all the extra time on the food, leaving none for the host or hostess to marinate in a nice hot tub or for festive table laying. So the menus that follow are a little bit special. Each should take, all told, no more than 45 minutes to prepare and most of them give you that 10–15 minutes of peace and quiet before serving that allows you to compose yourself as well as the meal.

MENU

Gorgonzola, Pear and Walnut Salad

———

Salmon and Crab Timbales

———

Cucumber and Orange Hollandaise Sauce

———

Hot Brioche Pudding

This is really a summer menu although the ingredients are available all year round. It's a light and delicate meal starting with a salad and finishing with a delicious citrus flavoured pudding. Although the timbales may sound complicated they are simplicity itself and sure to produce the requisite 'ooh-aah' from impressed guests.

The *Salmon and Crab Timbales* can be made in specially designed little aluminium moulds but I find that large teacups work equally well and have the advantage of a handle to help lift them out of the water. Either way, this is the crafty way of making fish mousses. You may well read in some French chefs' books about the need for hours of beating over bowls filled with ice. Forget it. Relax and enjoy one of the more exotic ways of eating fish. To remove the smaller bones in the salmon, use a pair of sterilised tweezers.

LEFT
Hot Brioche Pudding
(see page 119)

BELOW LEFT
Salmon and Crab Timbales
(see page 119)

BELOW
Gorgonzola, Pear and Walnut Salad
(see page 118)

Gorgonzola, Pear and Walnut Salad

SERVES 4 AS A STARTER

1 x 150 g/5 oz bag mixed salad leaves
100 g/4 oz walnut halves
100g/4 oz Gorgonzola cheese
1 ripe red-skinned pear
1 tbsp lemon juice
1 tsp sugar
½ tsp salt
1 tbsp red wine vinegar 🛒 (see page 16)
2 tbsp walnut oil 🛒
2 tbsp sunflower oil
warm crusty bread, to serve

Arrange the salad leaves in a large bowl. Roughly crush three quarters of the walnuts and mix through the salad leaves. Cut the Gorgonzola into 1 cm/ ½ in squares. Peel and core the pear, cut into thin slices, toss in the lemon juice and set aside. Sprinkle the salad with the sugar and salt and then the red wine vinegar and toss. Add the walnut and sunflower oils and toss once again. Do not do this more than 10 minutes before you are ready to eat, or it can be done at the very last minute. Just before serving sprinkle the salad with the Gorgonzola and arrange the remaining walnut halves and the pear slices over the top. Serve with the warm crusty bread.

NUT OILS

As well as basic cooking oils like olive or sunflower, you can buy special oils with a considerable amount of flavour, the most generally available being walnut, hazelnut and sesame. They are usually sold in small bottles and most supermarkets and speciality stores stock them.

Walnut oil is much used, particularly in France and in Italy, as a salad dressing where it imparts the flavour of the nut to the vegetables or salads that are being dressed. It does not keep well, so once opened should be stored in a cool place.

Hazelnut oil can be used similarly for lighter salads and is used by vegetarians to flavour vegetables as part of a hot dressing instead of butter.

Sesame oil is an integral ingredient of Chinese or oriental cooking and in this form has already been roasted before being pressed. Use it towards the end of cooking to season stir-fry dishes and add in small quantities to oil that is being used to deep-fry such things as tempura.

Salmon and Crab Timbales

SERVES 4

750 g/1½ lb salmon fillets, skinned
2 tbsp sunflower oil
3 eggs
seasoning
juice of half a lemon
2 spring onions, trimmed and finely chopped
100 g/4 oz fresh or canned white crab meat
1 tbsp finely chopped fresh parsley
boiled new potatoes, to serve

Cut the salmon into 2.5 cm/1 in cubes and put it with the oil, the eggs and a generous seasoning of salt and pepper into a food processor. Process until smooth. Add the lemon juice and process again. Line 4 × 10 cm/4 in × 7.5 cm/3 in dariole moulds or large teacups with oiled clingfilm. Spoon in enough salmon mixture to half fill each cup, making a slight indentation to allow the salmon mixture to come up the sides. Mix the spring onions with the parsley and crab meat. Divide this mixture between the dariole moulds ensuring it is completely enclosed by the salmon mixture. Top with the remaining salmon mixture and place the moulds or teacups in a frying pan with 4 cm/1½ in of water. Cover with a lid and bring to the boil. Simmer for 10–12 minutes until the salmon timbales are risen and firm to the touch. To serve, invert each timbale, open side down, onto a warmed plate and lift the mould or teacup carefully, peeling off the clingfilm as you do so. Serve with new potatoes and the *Cucumber and Orange Hollandaise Sauce*.

Crafty Tips

● This whole menu can be prepared uncooked up to 4 hours in advance.

● The *Salmon and Crab Timbales* can be frozen, uncooked, for up to 3 months.

Cucumber and Orange Hollandaise Sauce Ⓥ

MAKES ABOUT 150 ML/¼ PINT

120 ml/4 fl oz Hollandaise Sauce (see recipe page 22)
¼ cucumber, halved, seeded and diced
juice of half an orange

Place the hollandaise sauce in a small pan and just heat through. Stir in the cucumber and orange juice and warm through without allowing to come near the boil. Serve with the salmon and new potatoes.

Hot Brioche Pudding

SERVES 4

50 g/2 oz raisins
4 brioche buns
75 g/3 oz butter, plus extra for greasing
50 g/2 oz candied mixed peel, cut into small pieces
2 eggs
300 ml/½ pint milk
75 g/3 oz caster sugar
1 tsp vanilla essence
icing sugar, to dust

Preheat the oven to 180C/350F/Gas 4/160C fan (middle of the Aga roasting oven). Scatter the raisins into a shallow buttered dish about 25 cm/10 in in diameter. Cut each brioche bun into four slices. Melt the butter in a large frying pan and fry the brioche slices on both sides for a couple of minutes until golden. Tip into the dish with any remaining buttery juices and scatter the mixed peel on top. Whisk together the eggs, milk, sugar and vanilla essence and pour evenly over the pudding. Bake for about 25 minutes until risen and golden. Serve warm dusted with icing sugar.

MENU

Pinwheels of Smoked Trout

—

Chicken Chasseur

—

Spiced Pear Compote

A menu really for winter or at least autumn – rich and warming, making use of the kind of produce like mushrooms and pears that are at their best in the closing months of the year. It's French in tone, though if you go back about a hundred years, the recipes are very similar to those that were traditionally eaten in great English country houses.

Literally translated *Chicken Chasseur* means 'hunter's chicken' but in fact it is chicken cooked in the autumnal-style with mushrooms in a creamy sauce. Boiled rice or, my favourite, mashed potatoes are the perfect accompaniment with a crunchy, elegant green vegetable like mangetout peas, broccoli florets or French beans.

The *Spiced Pear Compote* is a simple and delicious way of eating our English conference pears. Buy pears that are still hard, or at least have not become really soft and bruised.

Pinwheels of Smoked Trout

SERVES 4 AS A STARTER

100 g/4 oz cream cheese
1 tbsp chopped fresh dill
2 tbsp snipped fresh chives
freshly ground black pepper
100 g/4 oz packet smoked trout slices
½ small cucumber, cut into matchsticks
salad leaves and lemon wedges, to serve

Mix together the cream cheese, dill, half the chives and a little pepper in a bowl. Reserve four of the best pieces of trout and finely chop the remainder and stir it into the mixture. Lay out the reserved trout slices and spread a quarter of the cream cheese mixture over each slice. Carefully roll up the trout, neatly trim off the ends and slice each into three. Arrange on serving plates and garnish with black pepper and the remaining chives. Serve with the cucumber sticks, salad and lemon wedges.

Chicken Chasseur

SERVES 4

2 tbsp softened butter
1 tbsp vegetable oil
4 chicken breast fillets, skinned
1 large onion
250 ml/8 fl oz chicken stock or apple juice
    (or a mixture of both)
1 bouquet garni (stick of celery, sprig of
    parsley and thyme and a bay leaf tied
    together)
225 g/8 oz chestnut or button mushrooms 🛒
    (see page 66)
1 heaped tbsp plain flour
150 ml/¼ pint single cream
seasoning
rice or mashed potatoes and green vegetables

Pinwheels of Smoked Trout

Melt half the butter and the oil together in a large pan until the butter stops sizzling. Add the chicken and fry gently for about 5–6 minutes until golden on both sides. Peel and finely chop the onion, add to the pan and fry for another 4–5 minutes until softened. Pour in the stock and/or apple juice and add the bouquet garni, cover and simmer for about 10–15 minutes, turning the chicken once until it is completely cooked through. Check this, if you like, by piercing the chicken with a skewer and making sure that the juices run clear.

Trim and wipe the mushrooms clean. If they're large, split them into halves or quarters. Remove the chicken from the pan with a slotted spoon and keep warm. Add the mushrooms to the pan and simmer for 2 minutes while you combine together the remaining tablespoon of butter and the flour to make a beurre manié. Do this with a fork on a saucer. Remove the bouquet garni and stir the beurre manié forkful by forkful into the sauce and bring it to the boil. It will thicken and go glossy and delightfully shiny. Season to taste, stir in the cream and return the chicken to the pan just to heat through. Serve in the pan if it's attractive or arrange the chicken on a serving dish and pour the sauce over it.

Spiced Pear Compote

SERVES 4

4 large ripe conference pears
juice of half a lemon
2 pieces of stem ginger plus 2 tbsp of the syrup
1 tbsp water
¼ tsp ground mace or freshly grated nutmeg
25 g/1 oz caster sugar (optional)
sprig of rosemary
50 g/2 oz toasted hazelnut pieces
single cream, to serve

Peel and core the pears, cut into 2.5 cm/1 in pieces and sprinkle with the lemon juice to prevent them turning brown. Place in a non-stick pan with the ginger syrup and the water. Sprinkle with the mace or nutmeg and, if the pears need it, up to 25 g/ 1 oz of caster sugar. Add the sprig of rosemary, cover and simmer for about 10 minutes or until the pears are just cooked through but not collapsed. Meanwhile, chop the stem ginger and hazelnuts together. Remove the rosemary from the pan, spoon the pears into serving dishes and sprinkle the ginger and hazelnut mixture on top. Drizzle over a little cream and serve warm or cold.

Crafty Tips

● The *Pinwheels of Smoked Trout* and *Spiced Pear Compote* can be made up to 12 hours in advance. Cover and chill until ready to serve.

● The *Chicken Chasseur* can be made up to the stage of adding the cream. Cover and chill, then reheat gently but thoroughly, add the cream and finish cooking.

● The *Chicken Chasseur* (prior to adding the cream) is suitable for freezing for up to 3 months.

STEM GINGER
As well as being available fresh, powdered, or ready-crushed in jars, ginger also comes crystallised as an exotic sweetmeat and preserved in syrup in jars, usually in balls about the size of a large marble. This very useful spice is thought to be a very good preservative and is also helpful in relieving digestion problems.

Garlic Cheese Mushrooms

—

Cod with Tomatoes and Sweet Peppers

—

Mocha Baked Alaska

Shopping is crucial to this very simple and light menu, as it requires a number of prepared ingredients. This is a particularly pretty meal as the cod, cooked, almost steamed, on top of its delicious tomato and pepper sauce, has a lovely pristine clearness to it that looks marvellous. A dish of plain boiled rice goes very well with it or, if you prefer it, new potatoes. It doesn't need another vegetable.

The key to the starter is the herb and garlic cream cheese that you can find in cheese shops or on supermarket cheese counters. The different varieties are all excellent in flavour and as all the work's been done for you, there is enough time to stuff a mushroom.

Garlic Cheese Mushrooms

SERVES 4 AS A STARTER

4 large or 8 medium-sized open cup
   mushrooms
50g/2 oz fresh white breadcrumbs
100 g/4 oz garlic herb cream cheese (a good
   brand)
1 egg
crusty French bread, to serve

Preheat the oven to 180C/350F/Gas 4/160C fan (middle of the Aga roasting oven). Put the mushrooms, with their detached stalks, in a colander. Pour a kettle of boiling water over the stalks and caps to clean and sterilise them. Put the caps aside to drain, and chop the stalks. Mix them with the breadcrumbs, the cheese and the egg until the mixture is smooth. Place the mushroom caps in a baking dish which you have lightly oiled and spoon the mixture into them, sharing it equally between them. Bake in the oven for 15–20 minutes until the filling is set and the mushrooms are cooked through. Serve with plenty of French bread to mop up all of the delicious juices.

HERB CREAM CHEESE
You can purchase herb cream cheese in both branded and bulk packaging. The branded ones usually have a French name, like Boursin, and have both a full and reduced fat version. The bulk variety are sold in logs that look like Swiss Rolls that have herbs in layers between the cheese. This is usually sold in slices. Flavours vary slightly from variety to variety.

LEFT
Mocha Baked Alaska
(see page 126)

BELOW LEFT
Garlic Cheese Mushrooms
(see page 123)

BELOW
Cod with Tomatoes and Sweet Peppers
(see page 126)

Cod with Tomatoes and Sweet Peppers

SERVES 4

4 tbsp olive oil (see page 15)
225 g/8 oz Spanish onions, peeled and thinly
   sliced
1 small red pepper, seeded and sliced
1 small yellow pepper, seeded and sliced
1 x 400 g/14 oz can chopped tomatoes
1 tbsp chopped fresh thyme or 1 tsp freeze-
   dried thyme (see page 53)
½ tsp dried chilli flakes or chilli powder
juice of 1 small lemon
4 x 175 g/6 oz cod steaks
seasoning
chopped fresh parsley, to garnish
steamed new potatoes or rice, to serve

Heat the oil in a large frying pan, add the onions
and cook them gently for 3–4 minutes until they're
softened but not browned. Add the peppers and
cook for another 2–3 minutes. Add the tomatoes,
thyme, chilli and the lemon juice. Bring to the boil,
season generously, cover and simmer for about 5
minutes, stirring occasionally until the mixture has
thickened slightly. Place the pieces of cod on top
of the tomato mixture, cover the pan tightly and
simmer for about 10–12 minutes until the fish is
steamed through. You will be able to tell this
because it will have taken on a marvellous snow-
white opacity. Garnish with parsley and serve with
steamed potatoes or rice. The combination of
colours and flavours is stunning.

Mocha Baked Alaska

SERVES 4

175 g/6 oz chocolate sponge (shop bought or
   home made)
2 tsp instant coffee
2 egg whites
100 g/4 oz caster sugar
½ litre round tub coffee or vanilla and
   chocolate flake swirl ice-cream
   (see page 41)

Preheat the oven to 220C/425F/Gas 7/200C fan
(top of the Aga roasting oven). Cut the chocolate
sponge into slices and use to line a 20 cm/8 in
sandwich cake tin. Mix the coffee with a tablespoon
of boiling water and sprinkle over the sponge. Whisk
the egg whites in a clean, grease-free bowl until
stiff. Whisk in half the sugar, a tablespoon at a time,
then fold in the remaining sugar. Loosen the sides
of the ice cream in the tub, tip it into the sandwich
tin and press out gently to fill the base. Spread the
meringue over the top and sides of the ice cream
to coat it completely, making sure there are no
gaps, then rough up with a fork. Bake for about 10
minutes or until the meringue is golden. Serve at
once by cutting into slices.

Crafty Tips

● You can prepare the *Garlic Cheese Mushrooms*
uncooked up to 12 hours in advance.

● The sauce for the cod and the base for the
dessert can also be made up to 12 hours in
advance. Simply cover and chill until ready to finish
cooking.

● The sauce for the cod and the uncooked cod
steaks can be frozen separately for up to 3 months.

MENU

Courgette Remoulade

———

Steak with Anchovy Butter

———

Sicilian Cheesecake

Courgette Remoulade

SERVES 4 AS A STARTER

450 g/1 lb courgettes
6 tbsp Mayonnaise (bought or see recipe page 15)
2 tsp Dijon mustard 🛒 (see page 15)
25 g/1 oz (about 3) cocktail gherkins
1 tbsp capers
1 tbsp chopped fresh parsley
few drops of lemon juice (optional)
seasoning
lettuce leaves, to serve

Top and tail the courgettes and grate them as coarsely as possible or use the julienne shredder in your food processor. Mix together the mayonnaise and mustard. Finely chop the gherkins and capers and add with the parsley to the mayonnaise mixture. Check for seasoning. You may like to add a drop or two of lemon juice depending on how sharp the mayonnaise is. Mix the mayonnaise, which is now called a remoulade sauce, into the grated courgettes and mix thoroughly. Add seasoning to taste. Line individual bowls with a few lettuce leaves and spoon a heap of the remoulade into the middle. Do not make this more than 30 minutes before you are going to eat as the courgettes can lose liquid and make the whole thing rather runny.

Here's a meal that could be described as opulent – it's certainly got some grand ingredients. But although it is rich it is not cloying. As always, it's worth being particular about the quality of the ingredients. As the courgettes are being eaten uncooked, look for ones that are firm and glossy-skinned. This dish is a modern, light adaptation of a dish normally made with celeriac. As courgettes are available all year round, and are delightful eaten raw, this is an excellent alternative. For the crystallised fruit in the pudding you could use mixed peel designed for baking but an investment in a small amount of high quality crystallised fruit makes the most amazing difference.

Steak with Anchovy Butter

SERVES 4

75 g/3 oz softened butter
25 g/1 oz Gentleman's Relish (anchovy paste
     with some seasonings)
juice of half a lemon
a little sunflower oil
4 × 175–225 g/6–8 oz steaks (fillet or sirloin)
     at least 2.5 cm/1 in thick
watercress sprigs, to garnish
fresh green salad, to serve

Mix together the butter and the Gentleman's Relish
in a bowl until it forms a smooth mixture. Add the
lemon juice and mix well. Place the mixture on to a
piece of kitchen foil and shape into a rough
sausage. Roll the foil up and make the sausage as
neat as possible by rolling it under your hand. Put
in the fridge to chill. When ready to cook the steaks,
preheat your grill for at least 10 minutes, brush the
preheated grid of the grill with a little oil and place
the steaks on it. Grill 5 cm/2 in away from the heat
for 2 minutes a side for rare, 3 minutes a side for

STEAK
The way in which beef is hung has a major
influence on its eating texture. As steak
cooks so quickly it's a dish that clearly
shows up the quality of the meat. A lot of
meat, though it may be technically steak
cuts, is not at all nice to eat in a simple
grilled form. My advice is to look for beef
that has the Aberdeen Angus or Scottish
Beef sign on it or one that has been
labelled 'traditional'. The Q Guild of
butchers specialise in high quality beef
that's been hung for long enough to
mature and develop a proper flavour.

---

medium and 4 minutes a side for well done. Remove
the steak from the pan, put onto warm plates,
garnish with a few watercress sprigs and slice the
anchovy butter into 1 cm/½ in pats, placing two on
each steak to melt over it and provide the sauce.
Serve at once with the salad and the *Rosti*.

Rosti

SERVES 4

750 g/1½ lb potatoes
1 tbsp grated onion
25 g/1 oz self-raising flour
1 egg
4 tbsp sunflower oil

Peel the potatoes and grate them finely – a food
processor helps with this. Press the mixture firmly
in your hands and blot with kitchen towel to remove
excess liquid, then mix in a bowl with the grated
onion, the flour and the egg. In a large frying pan,
heat the oil and, dividing the mixture into four, make
four oval-shaped patties and place these in the hot
oil. Cook gently for about 6 minutes on each side
until golden brown and cooked through. Serve
immediately with the steak. You may also wish to
serve a green salad with or immediately after
the steak.

Sicilian Cheesecake (see page 130)

Sicilian Cheesecake

SERVES 4

In its native Sicily this is known as Cassata, not an ice-cream confection but a rather fancy cheesecake. In this crafty version I've made it as simple as possible without losing any of the delicious flavours. You will need to find ricotta, the Italian version of cottage cheese. In this recipe cottage cheese won't substitute.

1 × 20 cm/8 in sponge cake, home-made or bought
6 tbsp fresh squeezed orange juice **(see page 21)**
100 g/4 oz caster sugar
2 tablespoons water
350 g/12 oz ricotta cheese
pinch of ground cinnamon
225 g/8 oz crystallised fruit
50 g/2 oz dark bitter chocolate, chopped into slivers
icing sugar, to decorate

Cut the sponge cake horizontally into two. Place the bottom half on a serving dish and sprinkle with four tablespoons of the orange juice. Put the caster sugar into a pan with the water, bring to the boil and stir until completely dissolved. Allow to cool a little and beat into the ricotta with the cinnamon. Mix until completely smooth. Roughly chop the crystallised fruit leaving one or two of the cherries in quite large pieces. Mix 175 g/6 oz of the fruit into the ricotta with half of the chocolate. Spread the filling over the bottom half of the sponge cake, add the top half of the sponge cake and sprinkle that in turn with the remaining orange juice. Press down gently to make sure it's firm without squeezing all the filling out. Decorate with icing sugar and the reserved crystallised fruit and chocolate. Chill for up to 2 hours before serving. Bring it to the table on as grand a platter as you have and serve it cut like a cake.

Crafty Tips

● The *Courgette Remoulade* can be prepared up to 4 hours in advance. Cover and chill until ready to serve.

● The *Anchovy Butter* and *Sicilian Cheesecake* can be made up to 24 hours in advance. Cover and chill until ready to serve.

CRYSTALLISED FRUIT
You will find this in many forms, including whole pineapples and peaches, but for this recipe you need the sort of crystallised fruit that's designed to be cooked with. It can often be bought in supermarkets or loose in specialist confectionery shops and should include bits of pineapple, cherries, plums and peaches. At a pinch you can use chopped mixed peel but it's not as nice and even when at its freshest lacks the variety that a range of crystallised fruit gives.

4

SEASONAL ENTERTAINING

Entertaining for seasonal celebrations is particularly satisfying. Whether it's a warming meal for one of the autumn celebrations, such as Hallowe'en or bonfire night, or entertaining American friends at Thanksgiving, one feels justified in going to town a little on the food.

I have enlivened some of the more traditional dishes with some unusual flavours so that you can serve up something unique to your family and friends. There is also a Christmas planner to keep the work, at that particularly busy time, to an absolute minimum.

FOOD AND DRINK

CHRISTMAS LUNCH

For the Christmas cook the workload seems enormous, even for quite a small group of people. But it's still possible to make Christmas lunch a very easy meal. The great trick is in the preparation. Two lots of two hours spent during the three days before Christmas make all the difference on the day. My presumption behind the planning is that you will want to have something resembling a traditional Christmas meal but with a dash of Eastern promise ... a delicious, spicy prawn starter, a turkey recipe with a twist, traditional Christmas vegetables made a bit more interesting, and a choice of Christmas cake, pudding, mince pies and chocolate and hazelnut tart, all of which can be made at the last minute. To give yourself maximum time out of the kitchen on the big day see 'The Christmas Organiser' on page 145.

Thai Prawn and Mango Salad

SERVES 6–8 AS A STARTER

This is a tropical dish on a midwinter's day, but why not? In recent years the clear, bright, sharp spices of Thailand and its cooking have turned out to be firm favourites with the British palate. They are applicable to all sorts of recipes and ingredients but it may come as a bit of a shock to know that they are also delicious at Christmas time.

150 g/5 oz bag mixed salad leaves
10 cm/4 in piece of cucumber
1 large mango
juice of 1 lime 🛒 (see page 38)
1 tsp caster sugar
seasoning
4 tbsp sunflower oil
25 g/1 oz butter
1 garlic clove, peeled and crushed
2 tsp Thai red curry paste
450 g/1 lb large cooked peeled prawns,
    defrosted if frozen 🛒 (see page 57)
2 tbsp chopped fresh coriander

Arrange the salad leaves in a large salad bowl. Cut the cucumber in half, scoop out the seeds and cut into slices. Peel the mango and cut into thin slices, discarding the stone. Scatter the cucumber and mango over the salad leaves, cover with clingfilm and chill until ready to serve. To make the salad dressing, mix together the lime juice, sugar, seasoning and oil in a small bowl, then chill. Melt the butter in a large frying pan and fry the garlic for 30 seconds. Stir in the curry paste, toss in the prawns and cook until just heated through. Tip the cooked prawns over the salad mixture, sprinkle with the coriander and serve at once.

Thai Prawn and Mango Salad

Thai Turkey

**SERVES 6–8 WITH ENOUGH LEFTOVERS
FOR BOXING DAY**

If you'd like a more traditional turkey recipe then turn to page 181. But Thai flavours can also ring the changes on the traditional turkey. I suspect this is an adult taste, although older children do seem to enjoy it enormously. Eaten with the unusual variety of slightly spicy vegetables, it certainly gives plain turkey, mashed potatoes and sprouts a new direction. In this recipe you can use either puréed or fresh flavourings – I will give both measurements. The ingredients are given for a 5.5 kg/12 lb turkey and need to be varied if you have one that is smaller or much larger. The turkey would benefit greatly from marinating in its spices for 12–14 hours before roasting.

2 stalks (about 7.5 cm/3 in long) **fresh lemon grass**, finely chopped, or 2 heaped tbsp crushed lemon grass 🛒 (see page 57)
2 large cloves of **garlic**, crushed, or 2 tsp crushed garlic (from a jar)
2.5 cm/1 in piece fresh **ginger** or galangal (Thai ginger), peeled and finely chopped, or 2 heaped tsp ginger purée 🛒 (see page 68/122)
3 red **chillies**, seeded and finely chopped, or 2 level tsp crushed red chilli
2 tbsp chopped fresh **coriander**
1 tbsp **sunflower oil**
grated rind and juice of 2 **limes**, plus 1 extra whole lime 🛒 (see page 38)
5.5 kg/12 lb **turkey**, defrosted if frozen
900 ml/1½ pints **hot water**
lime wedges, to garnish
Gravy, Lime and Honey Parsnips, Broccoli Mimosa, Garlic and Chilli Potatoes, to serve (see recipes right and overleaf)

If you have a frozen turkey it is essential that it is defrosted in a cool place, and that sufficient time is allowed for this. It will take at least 48 hours for a bird of this weight for safety and flavour. If using

the fresh flavourings, place the lemon grass, garlic, ginger, chillies and coriander in a food processor or liquidiser with the oil and blend to a rough purée. Add the lime rind and juice.

Loosen the breast skin of the turkey by pinching it all over. Lift it up and smooth over 1–2 tablespoons of the puréed mixture under the skin and into the flesh, particularly across the breast and the thighs of the bird if you can loosen the skin that far. Smooth another tablespoon of the mixture inside the cavity of the turkey and smear the remainder all over the skin, paying particular attention to the places where you haven't managed to get under the skin. Cut the remaining lime into quarters and squeeze all over the turkey. Put the lime quarters into the bird's cavity and place the turkey on a non-metallic dish. Cover and leave to marinate for about 12 hours. Calculate the cooking time. You will need to roast it for 17–18 minutes per 450 g/1 lb and a previously frozen bird may need extra cooking time.

Preheat the oven to 180C/350F/Gas 4/160C fan (bottom of the Aga roasting oven). Place the turkey on a rack in a roasting tin and pour the hot water into the tin. Cover the bird with buttered papers or lightly oiled foil for the first half of the cooking time. Check that the bird is completely cooked by sticking a skewer or sharp knife into the thickest part of the thigh. If the juices run clear it's cooked, if they show any signs of pink it needs at least another 30 minutes and should then be checked again. When it's cooked, pour off the liquid into a pan. Wrap the bird in foil and leave for at least 15 minutes – this makes it easier to carve.

Once carved, garnish with wedges of lime.

For the gravy:
Thicken the turkey juices by mixing 1–2 tablespoons each of butter and plain flour to make a paste. Whisk into the boiling juices and simmer gently for 2–3 minutes until thickened.

Lime and Honey Parsnips (V)

SERVES 6–8

This is a delicious way of roasting parsnips with an exotic touch.

2 tbsp olive oil ⛒ (see page 15)
675 g/1½ lb parsnips, peeled and cut into
   thick chip-shaped pieces
1 tbsp clear honey
juice of 1 lime ⛒ (see page 38)
2 tbsp chopped fresh coriander or parsley
seasoning
lime wedges, to garnish

Preheat the oven to 180C/350F/Gas 4/160C fan (bottom of the Aga roasting oven). Heat the oil in a large roasting tin and when it's hot, add the parsnips, honey and lime juice. Stir well until the parsnips are thoroughly coated with the mixture. Season and roast for 35–40 minutes until lightly golden and caramelised – you will need to turn them halfway through cooking. Transfer them to a warmed serving dish and scatter with the chopped coriander or parsley. Garnish with the lime wedges to serve.

Broccoli Mimosa (V)

SERVES 6–8

This is an extremely pretty way of serving broccoli. It is derived from a Chinese recipe named after the flowering tree with pretty yellow flowers. The chopped egg against the dark green of the broccoli has a similar appearance.

1 hard-boiled egg
675 g/1½ lb broccoli, trimmed and cut into
   florets
50 g/2 oz butter
100 g/4 oz fresh white breadcrumbs
seasoning

Separate the white and yolk of the egg. Finely chop the white and rub the yolk through a sieve and set aside. Cook the broccoli in the usual way in a pan of boiling salted water for 7 minutes until bright emerald green and tender but not at all soggy. Drain it thoroughly, arrange in a serving dish and keep warm. Meanwhile, melt the butter in a frying pan, add the breadcrumbs, season and cook over a low heat until golden brown. Before serving, sprinkle the breadcrumbs over the broccoli and scatter over the egg white and then the yolk so that it resembles mimosa petals.

Garlic and Chilli Potatoes (V)

SERVES 6–8

This is a revelation. Even people who don't like spicy food can't get enough of potatoes cooked like this, so the quantities I give you are for 6–8 people under normal circumstances – although you may not find it's enough when they've tasted them.

1 kg/2 lb potatoes, cut into quarters (Desiree
   is a good variety for this)
2 large garlic cloves, peeled and crushed
1 tsp salt
2 tbsp crushed red chilli (from a jar) or thick
   chilli sauce
4 tbsp vegetable oil

Preheat the oven to 180C/350F/Gas 4/160C fan (bottom of the Aga roasting oven). Put the potatoes into a pan of cold salted water, bring to the boil and simmer for 6 minutes. Drain thoroughly. Mix together the garlic, salt and crushed chilli or sauce and coat the potatoes with it thoroughly. Leave for 10 minutes for the flavours to develop. Heat the oil in a roasting tin, turn the potatoes in the oil and roast for 45 minutes until cooked through and golden brown. Serve hot.

Chocolate and Hazelnut Tart

SERVES 6-8

This is an extraordinarily, pretty tart that seems to last about 30 seconds after you've put it on the table.

100 g/4 oz digestive biscuits
100 g/4 oz whole hazelnuts
75 g/3 oz butter, melted
50 g/2 oz light soft brown sugar
1 tsp ground cinnamon

For the filling:
150 g/5 oz bitter dark chocolate
75 ml/3 fl oz orange juice
1 × 7 g packet powdered gelatine or Gelazone
3 eggs, separated
250 g/9 oz mascarpone (Italian soft cheese) or substitute any British full fat cream cheese
whipped cream, whole toasted hazelnuts or grated dark chocolate, to decorate

Preheat the oven to 180C/350F/Gas 6/160C fan (top of the Aga roasting oven). Put the biscuits and hazelnuts into a food processor and blend until the mixture resembles fine breadcrumbs. Add the butter, sugar and cinnamon and mix thoroughly. Use to line the bottom and sides of a 20 cm/10 in loose-bottomed flan tin. Bake for 20 minutes then remove from the oven and leave to cool.

Break the chocolate into small pieces and melt in a heatproof bowl over a pan of hot water. Put the orange juice in a small, heavy-based pan, add the gelatine or Gelazone and stir thoroughly. Heat very gently until the gelatine or Gelazone has completely dissolved. Remove from the heat and beat in the melted chocolate and the egg yolks. Beat in the mascarpone cheese until the mixture is completely smooth. Whisk the egg whites in a bowl until they

are completely stiff and using a large metal spoon fold into the chocolate mixture. Spoon the mixture into the cooled biscuit case, spread until the top is smooth and chill for at least 4 hours. Decorate with whipped cream, whole toasted hazelnuts or grated bitter chocolate.

GELATINE
In the past, gelatine used to be very difficult to work with but now the vegetarian Gelazone or powdered animal gelatine makes it much easier to handle. You can, if you wish, soak them cold in the liquid they're going to be used in and then heat them through. But there's really no need anymore, particularly with the vegetarian version. They normally come in sachets, pre-measured and ready to use with the amount of liquid indicated. In the case of the *Chocolate and Hazelnut Tart*, however, trust my directions.

Chocolate and Hazelnut Tart

Wines for Christmas Dinner

'There are only two types of drink I would seriously consider to open proceedings on Christmas morning...'

My first instinct when considering which wines to choose to accompany Christmas dinner would be to aim low, go for good value and don't think of even cracking, let alone breaking, the bank. But then everybody's Christmas dinner is different. Mine is unavoidably focused on the children and the accompanying distractions of noise, excitement, whoopee cushions, party poppers and the haunting smell of gunpowder smoke from the crackers. Definitely not a time to draw the cork of something magnificent which you would certainly have no time to sit back and enjoy. But I've heard tell that Christmas for some people is different. Civilised. Elegant. Perfectly organised. And quiet. And for those lucky enough to be able to indulge themselves in peace, of course Christmas can provide the perfect excuse for serving extremely special wines. Were I to go for the no-expense-spared approach to the festive season's big meal, I'd choose a marvellous old Champagne for starters, put on a top flight red Burgundy or the best Pinot Noir the West Coast of America can come up with – such as Robert Mondavi's Reserve Pinot Noir – or possibly a marvellous mature Northern Rhône red such as an Hermitage or a St Joseph and round off the meal with an unctuously gorgeous oloroso sherry such as Gonzalez Byass's Matusalem, which would go equally well with the Christmas pud as it would with a mature, subtle Stilton cheese. Dreams, just dreams.

In reality though, in common with the majority of Christmas revellers, I'm in the business of finding wines which I'm going to enjoy, but about which I will not break my heart if they are spilled or overpowered by the gunpowder smoke. Everyday-type wines with a spot more glamour.

THE APERITIF

There are only two types of drink I would seriously consider to open proceedings on Christmas morning: sparkling wine or fino sherry (two of my favourite drinks). They are both extremely festive, and light enough and streamlined enough to set your tastebuds tingling in expectation of the feast to come. Where sparklers are concerned, I must admit (unfashionably) that Champagne does things for me. Not just *any* Champagne – expensive though it is, regrettably even this luxury class of wine includes some damp squibs.

But many Champagnes are fine by me – including some at the bottom of the price range, because naïve though it sounds, even the label spells luxury. I'm also pretty excited by some of the marvellous – often more assertive on the flavour spectrum – sparklers coming out of the New World, with Australia, New Zealand and South Africa now being the key players.

If you want to lengthen the drink, Buck's Fizz is the obvious answer: 50/50 sparkling wine and orange juice is the recipe and for best results use fresh squeezed orange juice; carton concentrated types have a flavour of their own, somewhat divorced from the taste of real oranges. Even if you buy shop-prepared fresh squeezed juice 🛒 (see page 21) you'll see it makes all the difference. If you have guests for whom your sparkler is too dry, a drop or two of crème de cassis or blackcurrant syrup in the bottom of the glass friendlifies it a lot.

Fino sherry is the driest drink in the world (or should be!). Not to everybody's taste, I'll admit, but that gorgeous fresh, cleansing flavour is a brilliant appetite seducer. I would go

---

TO ACCOMPANY THE TURKEY

Reds:

● Pinot Noir from Chile (Cono Sur is particularly good).

● Zinfandel from California – now made as delicious berry-inspired light, juicy, fruity, reds.

● Crozes-Hermitage – less expensive, often more approachable cousin to Hermitage, the Northern Rhône's aristocrat, made from Syrah grapes.

● Cru Beaujolais made in, and named after, individual villages. Fleurie is over-priced now, but there are nine others to choose from (Brouilly, Chénas, Chiroubles, Côte de Brouilly, Juliénas, Morgon, Moulin-à-Vent, Régnier, St-Amour; expect good value from Côte de Brouilly and the newcomer Régniér).

Whites:

● Pinot Blanc from Alsace or Pinot Bianco from northern Italy.

● Viognier from southern France. Unusual Rhône grape variety making floral, soft, pretty whites in Languedoc named after the grape.

● Chenin Blanc from South Africa, friendly whites a couple of rungs up from the bottom of the sweetness scale.

● Mosel Riesling Kabinett – in the right hands Germany's top grape makes pretty, delicate off-dry wines with dashing acidity.

for one with an alcoholic strength of no more than 15.5 per cent (look for the strength on the label) and definitely chill it in the fridge – it can go in the previous evening – before serving. Manzanilla is also in the fino style, the only difference being that it is matured in a different town from other finos. Salted almonds are an ideal nibble to offer with fino.

WINES FOR TURKEY

Rules about matching wines with food are never more relaxed than when it comes to turkey. The big, festive bird doesn't even indicate the *colour* of the wine; it's almost a case of 'anything goes'. Oddly enough, one of the few exceptions I would make is claret. Although claret is the obvious Christmas dinner choice in the most traditional households, I would cite the austere, tannic reds of Bordeaux as one of the few wines that does *not* partner turkey very joyously.

If you tend to major on powerfully-flavoured trimmings to serve with turkey, red wine might have the edge over white; if, on the other hand, you are more of a plain cook catering for the whims of choosy children, I'd go for white. Dry white wine is fine, though I'd avoid the heavily oaked styles, but equally, softly medium-dry wines make good companions to Christmas dinner, too.

'Rules about matching wines with food are never more relaxed than when it comes to turkey.'

WHAT GOES WITH THE PUD?

Christmas pudding with brandy butter or brandy sauce present powerful enough flavours to walk all over delicate sweet wines. It's possible to inject a little sparkle into the proceedings at the end of the meal with some grapily sweet Asti Spumante, but, if you are up to it, I would recommend as first choice one of the delicious, intensely flavoured sweet wines made by Andrew Quady in California such as the dark red Elysium made from black muscat, like liquid Christmas pudding itself, or Essensia with its refreshing orange note. If these are hard to find, don't despair, Muscat de Beaumes de Venise is widely available and hits the spot, too. One surprise you perhaps hadn't bargained for is that sweet wines partner some cheeses very well, too, if you still have the appetite to continue your feast. Roquefort is the classic accompaniment, although other strongly flavoured types go well too. And of course there is no need to serve a different digestif; your luxuriously sweet dessert wine will do the job admirably.

FOOD AND DRINK

Vegetarian Mincemeat ⓥ

MAKES ABOUT 1.5 KG/3 LB

This recipe, which doesn't use animal fat, is delicious for Christmas mince pies. It's not the sort of mixture that keeps for months and months before you use it. It's absolutely best made in the days just before Christmas – it will keep comfortably in the fridge for a week.

450 g/1 lb cooking apples
250 ml/8 fl oz freshly pressed apple juice 🛒
 (see opposite)
225 g/8 oz sultanas
225 g/8 oz currants
225 g/8 oz raisins
50 g/2 oz butter
½ tsp ground cloves
1 tsp ground cinnamon
1 tsp ground nutmeg
50 g/2 oz light soft brown sugar
50 g/2 oz pecan nut halves
100 g/4 oz flaked almonds

Peel and core the apples, cut them into walnut-sized pieces and place in a pan with the apple juice. Cook for 5–10 minutes until they start to soften. Add the sultanas, currants, raisins, butter, spices and sugar, cover and simmer over a very low heat for 20 minutes. If the mixture starts to dry out, add a little more water to keep it moist (it should not be runny). Add the pecan nuts and almonds, and cook very gently for another 5 minutes. Stir thoroughly to prevent the mincemeat sticking. Allow to cool. Cover and chill until needed. It is now ready to be used for mince pies. You can either use pre-baked pie shells and fill them with the mincemeat, heating them in a very hot oven for just 5 minutes before you eat them, or you can make *Gilded Mince Pies*.

Gilded Mince Pies

MAKES 24 MINCE PIES

This way of decorating mince pies goes back to medieval times when very thinly beaten gold leaf was used. This method is not only more edible but also a great deal cheaper.

450 g/1 lb Vegetarian Mincemeat
 (see recipe, left)
450 g/1 lb ready-made puff pastry,
 defrosted if frozen 🛒
1 egg yolk
pinch of powdered saffron
whipped cream, to serve

Preheat the oven to 200C/400F/Gas 6/180C fan (top of the Aga roasting oven). Roll out half the pastry into a thin sheet. Cut out 24 × 7.5 cm/3 in rounds with a pastry cutter and use to line 24 tartlet tins. Spoon in the mincemeat to come two-thirds of the way up the sides. Roll the remaining half of pastry into another thin sheet and cut 24 × 6 cm/1½ in rounds to make lids. Dampen the edges of the filled pastry cases with a little water. Place a lid on each one, fitting them on and cutting a small slot in the top of each one. In a cup beat the egg yolk with the powdered saffron. Using a pastry brush, gild the lids with the yolk and saffron mixture and bake the pies for 25 minutes until the pastry is cooked and bright gold but not burned! Serve warm or cold with cream.

PUFF PASTRY
Ready-made puff pastry is sold by most supermarkets and delicatessens. It's simply much easier to buy than to make. You can now even buy it already rolled. The vegetarian puff pastries have a significantly reduced fat content.

Quick Mix Christmas Cake

MAKES ONE 20 CM/8 IN CAKE

This is a Christmas cake you can make just a couple of days beforehand. It's not as dark and heavy as traditional Christmas cake but some people may like it all the more for that. It still has plenty of rich flavour and a moist texture. It takes about 5 minutes to assemble although obviously, as with all cakes, longer to cook and cool. This is made in a food processor although you can, using soft margarine, do it quite quickly and easily by hand.

175 g/6 oz self-raising flour
2 eggs
75 g/3 oz softened butter
75 g/3 oz dark soft brown sugar
1½ tbsp milk
75 g/3 oz raisins
75 g/3 oz sultanas
75 g/3 oz mixed peel
25 g/1 oz toasted flaked almonds
(see page 70)
1 tsp ground mixed spice
1 tbsp dark treacle
grated rind and juice of 1 lemon
50 g/2 oz glacé cherries, halved

Preheat the oven to 160C/325F/Gas 2/150C fan (top of the Aga slow oven). Grease a 20 cm/8 in cake tin, and flour as well if it's not non-stick. Put the flour, eggs, butter, sugar and milk into a food processor and process for about 15 seconds. Scrape down the bowl and give it another whizz until the mixture is thoroughly blended. Add the dried fruit, almonds and spice, but not the cherries, and add the treacle, lemon juice and rind. Process for just 5 seconds to blend them in but not chop them up. Remove the knife carefully and pour the whole mixture into the cake tin. Arrange the cherry halves on top and bake for 2 hours. You may want to put a couple of butter papers over the top of the cake for the last 30 minutes or so if it starts to brown before the centre is set. Check to see it's cooked with a skewer, which should go into the middle and come out clean. It may need an extra 30 minutes cooking if the skewer is still smeary. Take the cake out of the oven and leave to cool for at least 4 hours on a wire tray. You can then turn it out either to eat as it is when it's completely cold or to ice in the traditional way.

APPLE JUICE

This comes in two significantly different styles. One is clear, rather like well-brewed tea to look at, and is always made from preserved, apple juice concentrate and then diluted with water. It's perfectly palatable but not a patch on freshly pressed apple juice which is always cloudy and pale, yellowy-green in colour. It has bits in it and has been neither strained nor concentrated, but normally has Vitamin C (ascorbic acid) added to give it a longer shelf life. You can find it in specific apple varieties, each with a different flavour and sharpness. These are really worth looking for as they are excellent to cook with and make the most delicious fruit drinks.

Last Minute Plum Pudding

MAKES ONE 1.5 LITRE/2½ PINT PLUM PUDDING

This is a simple version of the traditional Christmas pudding. This one can be made as late as Christmas Day if you wish. I suggest you mix and pre-cook it a little before that time, though, so that all you need to do on the day is reheat it. It's dark, rich and delicious and not quite so complicated as a traditional Christmas pudding.

175 g/6 oz plain flour
1 tsp salt
1 tsp baking powder
1 tsp ground cinnamon
1 tsp ground allspice
100 g/4 oz light soft brown sugar
100 g/4 oz fresh white breadcrumbs
100 g/4 oz candied peel
100 g/4 oz chopped mixed nuts (unsalted)
100 g/4 oz shredded suet (vegetarian is
   fine)
100 g/4 oz raisins
100 g/4 oz sultanas
3 eggs
1 tbsp black treacle
175 ml/6 fl oz milk
whipped cream, to serve

Place the flour, salt, baking powder, spices, brown sugar, breadcrumbs, candied peel, chopped nuts, suet, raisins and sultanas in a large bowl and mix well. In a separate bowl, put the eggs, treacle and milk and whisk together. Pour this into the dry ingredients and mix thoroughly until well combined. Put into a 1.5 litre/2½ pint buttered pudding basin and cover with a circle of non-stick silicone paper. Cover with foil with a fold in it and steam for 2 hours in a pan or for an hour in a pressure cooker.

If you wish to pre-cook the plum pudding and use it on Christmas Day, halve the steaming time and re-heat for 30 minutes in a pressure cooker or 1 hour in a saucepan or between 5 and 7 minutes in a microwave. Serve hot with whipped cream.

SUET

Originally suet was grated beef fat and indeed real suet still is. It has been an essential ingredient in things like Christmas pudding for centuries. Nowadays, however, there are supplies of vegetarian suet, similar in texture and cooking quality, but made usually in palm oil.

The Christmas Organiser

You can make your life easier next Christmas,
and for those that follow, by organising your time in the
kitchen as follows:

22 DECEMBER

If your turkey is frozen, take it out of the wrapper, remove the giblets and leave loosely covered in the fridge to defrost for at least 48 hours for safety and flavour.

23 DECEMBER

Make and bake the *Quick Mix Christmas Cake*. Leave to cool and mature slightly before you eat it on Christmas evening.

Make the *Last Minute Plum Pudding* and *Vegetarian Mincemeat*. Make the *Chocolate and Hazelnut Tart*, and freeze it.

24 DECEMBER –
CHRISTMAS EVE

Turkey: 14 hours before you plan to start roasting it, prepare the spices, cut out the wishbone to make carving easier and rub the spices over the bird. Leave to marinate in a cool place.

Lime and Honey Parsnips and Garlic and Chilli Potatoes: peel, cut into the size required. Put into separate china

or porcelain bowls with water acidulated with lemon juice.

Broccoli Mimosa: trim and cut the broccoli into florets. Place in a plastic bag and store in the fridge.

Thai Prawn Salad: arrange the salad leaves and mango in a salad bowl. Cover with clingfilm and chill until needed.

Make the *Gilded Mince Pies.*

25 DECEMBER –
CHRISTMAS DAY

Remove the *Chocolate and Hazelnut Tart* from the freezer 4 hours before you want to eat it.

Allow about 4 hours to cook the turkey.

Cook the vegetables.

Make the gravy.

Heat the *Last Minute Plum Pudding.*

New Year's Eve Buffet

This menu will provide a spectacular buffet for New Year's Eve or a similar festive occasion and comfortably feed a dozen people. You can, of course, double or increase the quantities depending on the number you choose to entertain. It is designed to be achievable in about 2½–3 hours. It doesn't take you much longer if you increase the quantities for a larger number of guests.

Liver Pâté

SERVES 12 AS A STARTER

Begin with a country-style liver pâté that can be cut in slices or simply spooned out of an attractive terrine onto hot French bread. Best made with calves' liver, you can substitute lambs' liver but the flavour is not quite as delicate.

1 onion, peeled and roughly chopped
1 garlic clove, peeled
750 g/1½ lb calves' liver, sliced and cut into
   cubes
50 g/2 oz butter, melted
2 eggs
1 tsp chopped fresh thyme
1 tsp chopped fresh tarragon
seasoning
hot French bread and *Sweet Onion Relish*
   (see recipe opposite), to serve

Preheat the oven to 350F/180C/Gas 4/1650C fan (bottom of the Aga roasting oven). Using a food processor, finely chop the onion and garlic. Remove from the processor but do not bother to wash the bowl. Put the liver in the food processor and process until smooth. Return the onion and garlic, and add the butter, eggs, herbs and seasoning. Process until the mixture is completely smooth. It will be quite runny. Pour it into a lightly oiled terrine or 1 kg/2 lb loaf tin. Place in a baking tray with 2.5 cm/1 in of boiling water all round it (properly called a bain marie) and bake for about 50 minutes until cooked through and firm to the touch. You may want to put a piece of foil or butter paper over the top of the pâté for the last 30 minutes of cooking to prevent it going crusty on the top. When it's cooked, allow the pâté to cool before removing from the tin or if it's cooked in a terrine you can serve directly from it. The pâté will be slightly pink in the middle and delicate and quite delicious. Serve it with plenty of hot French bread and the *Sweet Onion Relish*.

Lentil and Mushroom Pâté ⓥ

SERVES 12 AS A STARTER

This is an alternative vegetarian pâté everyone should enjoy. However, you may want to make both this and the liver pâté to satisfy all tastes.

225 g/8 oz green or brown lentils
50 g/2 oz butter
1 large onion, peeled and finely chopped
1 garlic clove, peeled and finely chopped
175 g/6 oz shiitake or chestnut mushrooms, washed and cut into quarters ⏢ (see page 66)
1 egg
1 tsp chopped fresh sage
1 tbsp chopped fresh parsley
1 tbsp chopped celery leaves
seasoning
hot French bread and *Sweet Onion Relish* (see recipe right), to serve

Preheat the oven to 180C/350F/Gas 4/160C fan (bottom of the Aga roasting oven). Put the lentils in a pan and add enough water to cover them by the depth of 4 cm/1½ in. Bring to the boil, skim and boil rapidly for 10 minutes, uncovered. Reduce the heat, cover and simmer for 15–20 minutes until they are soft but not disintegrating. Season well. In a separate pan, put the butter, onion, garlic and mushrooms and cook for 5–10 minutes until the onion is translucent and the mushrooms have given off some liquid. Drain the lentils carefully and put them in a food processor with the mushroom and onion mixture, egg, herbs and a generous amount of seasoning. Process until a smoothish purée is obtained. Pour into a loaf tin, pâté mould or terrine and bake in a bain marie roasting tin with 2.5 cm/ 1 in of boiling water all around it for about 30 minutes or until firm to the touch. Allow to cool before serving with hot French bread and *Sweet Onion Relish*.

Sweet Onion Relish ⓥ

SERVES 12

This is a most delicious addition, not only to pâtés but sandwiches and cold meats of all kinds. It will go with either pâté.

4 onions
2 tbsp sunflower oil
75 g/3 oz sugar
75 ml/3 fl oz red wine vinegar ⏢ (see page 16)
3 tbsp redcurrant jelly
150 ml/¼ pint red grape juice
seasoning

Peel the onions, cut in half and then cut into thin slices. Heat the oil in a large frying pan and stir in the onions. Cook over a very low heat, uncovered, for about 30 minutes, stirring frequently. Add the sugar, vinegar, redcurrant jelly and grape juice, and cook gently for another 30 minutes until well reduced and thickened. Season to taste, put into two small serving bowls and chill until ready to serve.

Baked Glazed Salmon

SERVES 12

Whole baked salmon is always a spectacular dish to present, but never more so than in the Christmas and New Year period when a surfeit of meat and fowl is usually the norm.

3–3.5 kg/7–8 lb whole salmon
a little sunflower oil
3 limes 🛒 (see page 38)
100 g/4 oz fine shred lime marmalade
1 tsp Tabasco or chilli sauce
Jewelled Rice Salad (see recipe right), to serve

Have the fishmonger prepare the salmon, or buy it ready-prepared as you can these days from the chill cabinet of a supermarket. You can remove the head if it troubles you but I think the nicest presentation is head on. Preheat the oven to 190C/375F/Gas 5/170C fan (middle of the Aga roasting oven). Lay out a piece of foil double the length of the salmon. Oil the foil and lay the salmon at one end of it. Cut up one of the limes into small pieces and use that to fill the cavity of the salmon. Fold the foil up carefully over the fish and fold into a neat seal without pressing down onto the flesh, so that there is an air pocket around the salmon. Lift it carefully onto a baking sheet and bake for 10 minutes per 450 g/1 lb. Remove from the oven and allow to cool on a flat surface.

Remove the foil and very carefully remove the skin from the salmon. You can remove most of the fins at the same time but leave the tail on. Gently melt the lime marmalade with the Tabasco or chilli sauce in a small pan and use this to carefully glaze the salmon with a couple of coats. Slice the remaining limes very thinly and lay these in an attractive pattern along the centre of the salmon, glazing a couple of times more with the lime jelly to set them. Place the fish on an attractive serving plate, give one last glazing and allow to cool completely. Set for at least 6 hours in the fridge before serving. Serve this as a centrepiece with

Jewelled Rice Salad, which could also be a vegetarian main course if required.

Jewelled Rice Salad

SERVES 12

Probably the prettiest salad you'll ever serve.

750 g/1½ lb long-grain or basmati rice
2 tsp salt
2 large yellow peppers, seeded
2 large red peppers, seeded
2 large bunches of spring onions, trimmed
4 tbsp olive oil 🛒 (see page 15)
100 g/4 oz skinned whole almonds
50 g/2 oz shelled pistachio nuts
juice of 2 lemons
50 g/2 oz glacé pineapple

Wash the rice in cold running water until the water runs clear. Put it into a large pan with half the salt, add enough water to cover it by at least 10 cm/4 in and bring to the boil. Cook for 8–10 minutes until just cooked through. Drain the rice well, then pour a jug of cold water through it and drain well again. Transfer to a large serving bowl. Chop the peppers and the spring onions into fine dice. Put half the olive oil in a frying pan and fry the peppers for 5–10 minutes until softened. Add the spring onions and cook for another minute, then add to the rice. In the same pan, fry the almonds and pistachio nuts until lightly golden and add to the rice mixture with the lemon juice and mix well. Cut the pineapple into small pieces and add with the remaining salt and olive oil, and mix together. The rice should have a jewelled appearance with the vegetables, fruit and nuts dotted through it. Chill until ready to serve with the Baked Glazed Salmon.

Jewelled Rice Salad

New Potato Salad with Dill Ⓥ

SERVES 12

Dill is a herb that has a natural affinity with potatoes and we're lucky enough to have new potatoes and fresh herbs available nearly all year round.

1.5 kg/3 lb small new potatoes
3 tbsp chopped fresh dill
75 g/3 oz mayonnaise (bought or see recipe page 15)
50 g/2 oz natural yoghurt
1 tsp lemon juice
1 tsp Dijon mustard 🛒 (see page 15)
1 tbsp clear honey
seasoning
tiny dill sprigs, to garnish

Place the potatoes in a large pan of boiling salted water and cook for about 10 minutes until completely tender. Drain and leave to cool a little. Meanwhile, mix together the dill, mayonnaise, yoghurt, lemon juice, mustard and honey in a large serving bowl. Season well. Stir the drained potatoes into the dill sauce while they are still warm, then chill thoroughly. Garnish with dill sprigs before serving.

Crafty Tips

● This whole menu can be made the day before, allowing you to ring in the New Year without any worries.

● Simply cover each dish with clingfilm and chill. Remove from the fridge about 30 minutes before you are ready to serve to allow everything to come back up to room temperature.

● You could reheat the *Peach and Cranberry Crumble* if you wanted to serve it warm. Just cover it with aluminium foil to prevent any further browning.

Peach and Cranberry Crumble

SERVES 10-12

Here's a pudding that can be served cold or hot.

6 large peaches or 2 × 400 g/14 oz cans peach halves in natural juice
450 g/1 lb fresh cranberries
150 ml/¼ pint water
½ tsp ground cinnamon
50 g/2 oz caster sugar
100 g/4 oz plain flour
100 g/4 oz chopped hazelnuts
100 g/4 oz butter
100 g/4 oz soft brown sugar
whipped cream or vanilla ice-cream, to serve 🛒 (see page 41)

Preheat the oven to 180C/350F/Gas 4/160C fan (bottom of the Aga roasting oven). If using fresh peaches, skin them by dipping into boiling water for 30 seconds, then peeling away the skin. Cut in half, remove the stones and cut the peach flesh into 1 cm/½ in dice. If using canned peaches, simply cut these in half and then dice them. Put the cranberries in a non-stick pan, add the water or the juice from one of the cans of peaches and the cinnamon and the caster sugar. Simmer for 10 minutes until the cranberries have become soft. Add the peaches, stir together and pour into a 2.25 litre/4 pint buttered, shallow pie or baking dish. Place the flour, hazelnuts, butter and brown sugar in a food processor and process until the mixture resembles breadcrumbs. Sprinkle this evenly over the top of the peach and cranberry mixture and bake for 40–45 minutes until the fruit is bubbling hot and the crumble is golden brown. Serve warm or cold with cream or ice-cream.

Peach and Cranberry Crumble

NEW YEAR'S EVE DINNER PARTY

Sometimes New Year's Eve is the opportunity for a sophisticated dinner party as opposed to the more exuberant forms of entertainment often adopted north of the wall that Hadrian built. This is a menu for such an occasion, chosen particularly as it represents, symbolically, some of the foods and concepts of the New Year – fresh herbs, seafood, pheasant and spiced apples are traditional in different cultures at this time of year. This menu should be achievable in about 45 minutes, depending on how organised you are. It includes a stir-fry and thus requiring some activity – albeit swift – in the kitchen at the last minute. You can buy 450 g/1 lb bags of frozen mussels which are shelled and cooked.

Baked Garlic and Herb Mussels

SERVES 4 AS A STARTER

The sort of dish that really should be eaten with a friend. The combination of flavours is intense and very satisfying.

75 g/3 oz butter
2 garlic cloves, peeled and crushed
2 tbsp chopped fresh herbs, such as a mixture of parsley, dill, chervil and fennel
juice of ½ lemon
225 g/8 oz cooked shelled mussels, defrosted if frozen
100 g/4 oz ready-made puff pastry, defrosted if frozen 🛒 (see page 142)
1 egg, beaten
seasoning
warm crusty French bread, to serve

Preheat the oven to 220C/425F/Gas 7/200C fan, (top of an Aga roasting oven). Place the butter, garlic, herbs, lemon juice and seasoning in the food processor and blend for 10 seconds. Scrape down the sides and whizz again until well blended. Divide the mussels into four 150 ml/¼ pint ramekins and spoon the garlic butter on top. Roll out the pastry on a lightly floured board and cut out four 10 cm/ 4 in rounds. Brush the edges of each ramekin with a little of the beaten egg, press the pastry rounds on top. Cut a small cross in the centre and brush with the remaining beaten egg. Bake for 10–12 minutes until the pastry is risen and golden brown. Serve at once with warm crusty French bread to mop up all the juices.

Pheasant à la Crème

SERVES 4

This dish uses the game bird with the most delicate flavour and succulent flesh. A hen pheasant is slightly smaller but many believe more delicious than a cock. It should feed 2–3 people so you'll need two for this dish. A fat cock would serve four on its own. The method of cooking used here ensures the pheasant cooks legs first, that the breast will not be overcooked, and there will be tasty juices to mix into the cream.

50 g/2 oz unsalted butter
2 hen pheasants, about 500 g/1½ lb each 🛒
1 onion, peeled and chopped
2 tsp small sprigs of thyme
300 ml/½ pint double cream
juice of ½ lemon
2 tsp Dijon mustard 🛒 **(see page 15)**
seasoning
Stir-Fried Fennel and Celery (see right) and
    creamy mashed potato, to serve

Heat the butter in a heavy-based pan with a tight fitting lid that will just hold the pheasants comfortably. Turn the pheasants in the hot butter until well coated and sealed. Add the onion and thyme, cover and cook over a moderate heat for 25 minutes, then remove the pheasants from the pan on to a plate. Pour in the cream and add the lemon juice, mustard and seasoning, and mix well. Return the pheasants to the pan, reduce the heat and cook for another 15–20 minutes until the pheasants are cooked through and tender. Remove the pheasants again, carve into quarters and keep warm. Bring the cream mixture to the boil and boil fast for 4–5 minutes, stirring continuously until thickened and slightly reduced. Season to taste and pour over the pheasant quarters. Serve at once with the Stir-Fried Fennel and Celery, and mashed potato.

Stir-Fried Fennel and Celery Ⓥ

SERVES 4

An excellent vegetable course in its own right, this very quick stir-fry has a nice palate-cleansing flavour as well as crispness to it.

225–350 g/8–12 oz bulb of fennel
225–350 g/8–12 oz head of celery
2 tbsp sunflower oil
½ tsp salt

Cut the bright green curly leaves off the fennel and remove the centre stalk leaves from the celery. Finely chop and put aside. Trim and wash the celery and fennel and cut across the grain into 5 mm/ ¼ in slices, discarding any damaged or stringy stalk. Heat the oil in a non-stick or well-seasoned wok or large frying pan and add the fennel. Stir-fry for 2 minutes over a high heat, then add the celery and continue cooking for 1–2 minutes until both are heated through but not soggy. Season with the salt and sprinkle with the leaves just before serving.

PHEASANT
Legally, pheasants have to be sold through game dealers but as all major supermarkets now have the licence you can buy very good pheasant, and other game, through them. Butchers also often have game dealer licences, so pheasant is easily bought at Christmas time when it's at its prime. Buy pheasant ready prepared and plucked but not wrapped in bacon or fat. A properly hung bird will have a flavour really rather like rich chicken and will not smell 'off'. This game bird can be casseroled, braised, sautéed and roasted.

RIGHT
Apple and Cinnamon Pudding
(see page 156)

LEFT
Pheasant à la Crème
with Stir-fried Fennel and Celery
(see page 153)

BELOW
Baked Garlic and Herb Mussels
(see page 152)

FOOD AND DRINK

Apple Cinnamon Pudding

SERVES 4

Wassailing for apples was one of the traditional Christmas and New Year activities. It often involved, so the story goes, attempting to pick up apples with the teeth while the fruit was floating in bowls of varyingly strong liquid. This recipe doesn't require any such dental dexterity but does maintain the idea of spiced apples as appropriate for the New Year. The brioche loaves can be bought from all sorts of speciality shops and supermarkets nowadays and are a light, sweet form of bread with a fine golden crumb.

**1 large brioche loaf
50 g/2 oz butter
2 eating apples, such as Cox's or another
    similar, scented variety** 🛒
**juice of 1 lemon
4 tbsp caster sugar
½ tsp ground cinnamon
¼ tsp ground cloves
pouring cream, to serve**

Preheat the oven to 200C/400F/Gas 6/180C fan (top of the Aga roasting oven). Cut 4 × 2 cm/¾ in slices from the brioche, discarding the two ends, and butter the slices on both sides. Arrange them in an overlapping layer in a shallow baking or roasting dish. Core the apples and cut each apple into six flat slices horizontally. Lay three pieces in a neat pattern on each slice of brioche and drizzle over the lemon juice. Mix together the sugar and spices and sprinkle over the top. Bake for 20–25 minutes. The fruit should be cooked through and the brioche browned but not burned. Serve warm with pouring cream.

Crafty Tips

● You can prepare the *Baked Garlic and Herb Mussels*, the *Stir-Fried Fennel and Celery* and the *Apple Cinnamon Pudding* ready to cook up to 12 hours in advance. Simply cover and chill until ready to use.

● The *Pheasant à la Crème* can also be cooked 12 hours earlier, jointed and left to cool, then re-heated later in its sauce in the pan. To serve, remove the joints to a serving dish and keep warm. Bring the sauce to the boil and boil fast for 1–2 minutes, whisking continuously. Pour over the sauce and serve at once.

● The *Baked Garlic and Herb Mussels* can be frozen for up to 3 months, providing the mussels or pastry weren't previously frozen.

APPLES
Particularly between August and February British apples are at their best. Early varieties include 'Discovery' and 'Worcester Pearmains'. In the middle of the season look for 'Cox's Orange Pippins' and 'Egremount Russets' and at the end of the season 'Kidd's Orange Red'.

SHROVE TUESDAY

Shrove Tuesday has a much more vivid and jollier name in French – Mardi Gras. We see Mardi Gras as carnival, an out-and-out festival of self-indulgence, dancing, singing and misbehaviour. But the phrase itself, from the Italian, actually means 'Meat Goodbye'! On the first day of Lent people gave up eating meat for forty days in Catholic Italy and France. So Shrove Tuesday was the day on which you used up all the goodies by making rich dishes, the kind of catch-all into which everything went. We still preserve a little of that tradition by eating pancakes on that day. I've chosen one Shrove Tuesday recipe from the United States where, if the austerity of Lent isn't always religiously observed, indulgence in these delicious pancakes certainly is. The Chinese Pancake Rolls make a perfect light supper, and both these dishes can be assembled in about 45 minutes.

Blueberry Pancakes

SERVES 4

American pancakes are smaller and fatter than those we eat in this country. Blueberries are scrumptious, and two or three of these pancakes, with a little cream or fromage frais, are superb as a weekend breakfast or pudding as well as for Shrove Tuesday of course.

150 g/5 oz plain flour
pinch of ground cinnamon
1 egg, beaten
25 g/1 oz butter, melted
150 ml/¼ pint milk
100 g/4 oz fresh blueberries (blackcurrants
 or redcurrants as an alternative)
2 tbsp vegetable oil
caster sugar and whipped cream, to serve

Whisk the flour and cinnamon with the egg, butter and milk to make a smooth batter. Thin down with a little water if necessary until the texture is that of a very thick double cream. Different flours will absorb different amounts of liquid. Leave to stand for 20 minutes in the fridge. Stir in the blueberries and heat a large, heavy-based frying pan. Dip a piece of kitchen paper into a saucer of vegetable oil and wipe the pan with the oil. Pour in tablespoonfuls of batter – a big pan will take 4 or 5 – and allow to spread to 7.5 cm/3 in size. Turn down the heat and let the pancakes set on one side for about 1½ minutes before flipping over. They will tell you when they're ready by small bubbles appearing on the surface. Cook for 1–2 minutes until lightly browned, stack on a warm plate and keep warm while you finish the batter. The mixture should make about 12–16 pancakes. Serve sprinkled with sugar and a dollop of cream.

Chinese Pancake Rolls

SERVES 4

These are really thin omelettes which are used to enclose a filling and are fried until crispy. I serve them with hoisin, chilli or soy sauce.

3 eggs
75 g/3 oz plain flour
75 g/3 oz cornflour
1 tbsp sunflower oil
pinch of salt
oil, for deep-frying

For the filling:
6 spring onions
1 tbsp sunflower oil
1 garlic clove, peeled and finely chopped
1 cm/½ in piece fresh root ginger, peeled and finely chopped 🛒 (see pages 68 and 122)
225 g/8 oz cooked peeled prawns 🛒 (see page 57)
1 tbsp soy sauce
½ tsp sugar
175 g/6 oz beansprouts, rinsed and dried
hoisin, chilli or soy sauce, to serve

Beat together the eggs, flour, cornflour, oil and salt until smooth. Stir in about 250 ml/8 fl oz of water until the batter is the consistency of thin cream. Leave to stand for 15 minutes. Whisk again until completely smooth. Use the batter to make 8 pancakes, leaving a little in the bottom of the bowl to use to seal the pancake rolls later. Heat a 20 cm/8 in frying pan, oil it lightly and pour in enough batter to cover the base of the pan in a thin layer, quickly swirling it around. Cook the pancake over a moderate heat until the edges curl and the top is set but not browned. Do not turn it over. Slide the pancake out of the pan on to a plate. Make 7 more pancakes.

To make the filling, trim the spring onions, keeping plenty of the green, and cut into a very fine dice. Heat the tablespoon of oil in a small pan and fry the garlic and ginger for 1 minute. Add the spring onions, prawns, soy sauce and sugar. Stir well and cook for 1–2 minutes. Add the beansprouts, turn for 30 seconds and place in a sieve to drain (the mixture needs to be very dry). Divide the filling into 8 portions. Place 1 portion in the middle of the uncooked side of a pancake. Fold up the bottom and fold in the sides and roll from the bottom upwards. Seal the top flap and ends with the remaining batter. Repeat with the remaining filling and pancake to make 8 pancake rolls. Deep-fry in batches in hot oil for 1–2 minutes until crisp and golden brown. Drain on kitchen paper and serve, two per person, with one of the sauces.

Crafty Tips

● The batter for the *Blueberry Pancakes* can be left to stand in the fridge, without stirring in the blueberries, for up to 12 hours.

● The pancake skins for the *Chinese Pancake Rolls* can be made up to 4 hours in advance. Separate with greaseproof paper, wrap in a polythene bag and keep in the fridge. You can also cook them completely, place on a baking sheet, then cover and chill for up to 12 hours. They can be re-heated for 10–15 minutes in the oven.

Blueberry Pancakes (see page 157)

EASTER LUNCH

Easter used to be, in food terms, a very special holy day in the year's calendar. Easter Sunday was the end of Lent and the end of fasting. In general terms this had been a no-meat diet for the previous 40 days and a considerable restriction on luxuries like cream and eggs. Therefore the Easter feast was, and in some families still is, a special event. Thus it's a time for family entertaining. This is a menu that reflects the Easter traditions of eggs, spring lamb and rich baking but which doesn't take long to prepare. The whole menu is meant to be achievable in about 2–2½ hours. The simnel cake needs to be cooked in advance if you want to decorate it because it has to cool. Preparing it and decorating it in the traditional way doesn't take long and using ready-made marzipan can be lots of fun, especially for the children.

Egg Drop Soup

SERVES 4–6 AS A STARTER

Although most eggs eaten at Easter these days are chocolate, the tradition of eating what had been for the whole of Lent a forbidden item was irresistible on Easter Sunday. This soup is very easy to make and has ancestors in both Italy and China. It's an ideal start to a celebratory occasion.

1 bunch of spring onions
1.2 litres/2 pints rich chicken stock
2 bay leaves
1 tbsp chopped fresh parsley, plus a couple of stalks
½ tsp salt
50 g/2 oz vermicelli
2 eggs
seasoning
thin slices of toasted French bread, to serve

Cut off the white part of the onions, roughly chop them and put them into a pan with the stock, bay leaves, parsley stalks and the salt. Bring to the boil and simmer for 10 minutes. Finely chop the green parts of the spring onions and set aside. Prepare the vermicelli according to packet instructions. Strain the stock and return to the pan with the softened vermicelli. Break the eggs into a bowl and beat them with a fork. Place a colander over the boiling stock and pour the beaten eggs, spoonful by spoonful, through the colander, so that they form drops as they pass through the holes. As soon as you have completed the exercise, turn the heat right down and add the green parts of the spring onions and the parsley. Season to taste and serve the soup immediately with lightly toasted French bread.

Egg Drop Soup

Shoulder of Lamb Braised with Spring Vegetables

SERVES 4-6

This is a novel version of the traditional French spring and Easter lamb dish – *Navarin Prantanier*. It's a bit more suitable for a special occasion as the lamb is cooked in one piece and sliced, but the marvellous way that the vegetables and the slightly sweet savouriness of lamb combine is as good as in the original French version. If your pocket will stand it, this may be an occasion to serve the first of the Jersey Royal new potatoes.

450 g/1 lb carrots
225 g/8 oz small turnips
450 g/1 lb leeks
2 tbsp olive oil 🛒 **(see page 15)**
225 g/8 oz asparagus tips 🛒
1 shoulder of lamb, boned (get your butcher
   to do this)
½ tsp dried rosemary
½ tsp dried thyme
1 garlic clove, finely chopped
seasoning
boiled new potatoes and redcurrant jelly, to
   serve

Preheat the oven to 190C/375F/Gas 5/170C fan (middle of the Aga roasting oven). Trim the carrots and turnips and thoroughly wash the leeks. Cut the leeks into 2.5 cm/1 in lengths, each of the turnips into eight wedges, and the carrots into halves lengthways. Gently fry the vegetables in the olive oil in a casserole or lidded roasting pan that will go comfortably in the oven. Add the asparagus tips and place the shoulder of lamb on top of the bed formed by all the vegetables. Season generously with salt and pepper and sprinkle with the herbs and garlic. Put the lid on or cover loosely with foil and bake for 25 minutes per 450 g/1 lb until the lamb is tender and the vegetables are lightly charred.

To serve, remove the lamb from the dish and carve it in the normal way (being boned makes this much easier). Stir the meat juices and the vegetables together, pouring off any excess fat that the meat may have produced. You can serve the vegetables as they are or puréed in a food processor or Mouli food press. Mint sauce won't go with the lamb, vegetables and boiled potatoes, but redcurrant jelly will (even though it's scarcely traditional in France!).

ASPARAGUS

Asparagus is now available in supermarkets and greengrocers all year round from different parts of the world. But nothing beats British asparagus in it's all too brief season from late May til mid July. You can often buy sprue which is the thinnings at very low prices. They are absolutely delicious.

Simnel Cake

SERVES 6

Simnel cakes, eaten traditionally at Easter, are supposed to be named after one of the most interesting minor characters in English history. Tudor England is littered with impostors, and Lambert Simnel, the son of an Oxford organ-maker, was one of them, used by the defeated Yorkists after the Wars of the Roses to try to de-throne Henry VII. He was a clever youth who was actually quite successful for a short time at convincing prominent Anglo-Irish lords in Ireland that he was the rightful king of England. The plot collapsed when, at the instigation of the Yorkist plotters, the Irish invaded and were defeated by Henry VII at a battle near Stoke. The first Tudor King has a reputation for meanness and parsimony – for which Simnel had much to be grateful. Instead of executing him (a clear waste of resources) Henry VII utilised him for years, as a cook in his kitchens. It was there that he created this cake, or one at least not too dissimilar from this. Traditionally it was covered in marzipan, or marchpane as it was called at the time. It was not iced but gilded with a little saffron water mixed into an egg yolk so it looked like a gold cake to eat on Easter Sunday. I just mix a little sugar and ground almonds together, thicken them with a little cream and use it as a soft topping just before the cake is eaten.

100 g/4 oz butter or baking margarine
100 g/4 oz caster sugar
2 eggs, beaten
175 ml/6 fl oz milk
175 g/6 oz plain flour
50 g/2 oz cornflour
2 tsp baking powder
50 g/2 oz ground almonds

For the topping:
50 g/2 oz ground almonds
2 tbsp caster sugar
4 tbsp double cream

Preheat the oven to 190C/375F/Gas 5/170C fan (middle of the Aga roasting oven). There are two ways of making this, in a processor or by hand. If you are making it by hand, cream together the butter and sugar with a wooden spoon until light and fluffy. Add the eggs and milk and then fold in the flour, cornflour, baking powder and almonds until well combined. If you are using a food processor, put all the ingredients in at once and give it a whizz. Make sure it is thoroughly blended. Put the mixture into a base-lined and greased 20 cm/8 in deep cake tin. Bake for about 1 hour. It will rise quite dramatically and be firm to the touch. Test with a skewer. If it comes out clean the cake is ready, if not return to the oven for another 5–10 minutes. Allow to cool for 5 minutes then remove from the tin and let it go completely cold. To make the topping, mix together the almonds and sugar until well combined. Stir in the cream and spread over the top of the cake, allowing it to dribble around the sides just before serving.

Crafty Tips

● You can make the *Egg Drop Soup* and prepare the *Shoulder of Lamb*, ready to go into the oven, up to 4 hours in advance. Cover and chill, removing the lamb from the fridge about 30 minutes before cooking to allow the meat to come back up to room temperature.

● You can also bake the *Simnel Cake* up to 24 hours in advance and decorate it once it has cooled.

● The *Simnel Cake*, without the topping, can be frozen for up to 3 months.

PICNICS

Picnics may be meals eaten in the open air but they don't have to be at the end of a long journey or in an exotic place. I often think the best ones are eaten in the garden or local park or even on the bank of a local stream or river.

I like picnics to have a certain practicality. Here I've devised two picnic menus which are easy to prepare, should be achievable in under an hour and are easily transportable.

The first picnic can even be eaten on the move with no need for extra kitchen utensils, except a sharp knife to cut the sandwiches. The second is more sophisticated and will need to be served on solid, disposable plates with cutlery provided. Both menus will happily serve four to six people.

Wherever you go, don't forget to take plenty of napkins, a pack of large wipes for hands, a rubbish bag and something hot to drink.

MENU

Smoked Salmon Fingers

—

Hunter's Omelette

—

Punjabi Chicken

—

Carrot Cookies

This is a menu that can be eaten while travelling. But the recipes are perfectly adaptable to more formal occasions. Take the *Smoked Salmon Fingers*, for example – real luxury picnic food but ridiculously easy to make. The *Hunter's Omelette* and *Punjabi Chicken* solve the problem of providing an interesting savoury picnic meal that isn't just an old-fashioned sandwich. The technique was developed in France where this style of bread originates. Finally, the *Carrot Cookies* make excellent picnic fare – chewy, crunchy and transportable.

Smoked Salmon Fingers (see page 166)

Smoked Salmon Fingers

SERVES 4–6

450 g/1 lb boneless salmon fillet
100 g/4 oz smoked salmon, thinly sliced
4 Peking duck-style pancakes
2 tbsp hoisin (plum) sauce

Ask your fishmonger to skin the salmon or remove it yourself using a very sharp knife and sprinkling the end of the fish you're holding with a little salt to prevent it slipping. Cut the fillet into eight equal finger-shaped slices. Divide the smoked salmon into eight pieces and wrap each raw salmon piece with a piece of smoked salmon. Place them on a lightly oiled heatproof plate that will fit inside your steamer or colander. Put about 5 cm/2 in of water in a pan and bring it to the boil. Place the steamer or colander on top, put the salmon on its plate inside and cover with a lid. Steam for 8–10 minutes until the salmon is opaque and just cooked through. Remove the plate from the pan and allow to cool.

Cut each of the pancakes in half, smear with a little of the hoisin sauce and wrap neatly around the bottom half of each of the fingers. Pack into a rigid airtight container and keep cool until ready to serve. To eat, hold the salmon by the pancake end and eat towards your fingers.

PEKING DUCK-STYLE PANCAKES
You can buy these in most major supermarkets as well as speciality Chinese shops. They are designed to be eaten with crispy roast duck, having been smeared with hoisin sauce and sprinkled with a little chopped spring onion and cucumber. The pancakes and sauce, however, enhance a wide range of other savoury snack foods.

Hunter's Omelette ⓥ

SERVES 4–6

1 × 45 cm/18 in French stick
25 g/1 oz butter, plus extra for spreading (optional)
2 tbsp mango chutney
1 bunch spring onions
175 g/6 oz courgettes
1 tbsp olive oil (see page 15)
4 eggs
seasoning

Cut the French stick in half lengthwise so that you have two canoe-shaped pieces and scrape out some of the crumb inside. If you like, you can butter the two canoe insides lightly but I don't usually bother. Spread half the mango chutney into each of them and, using the back of a spoon, make sure that there is some spread along the whole length of each piece of loaf. Trim and finely chop the spring onions, trim and grate the courgettes and press them in a sieve or colander with the back of your hand to get out as much liquid as you can. Fry the courgettes and onions in the olive oil until the courgettes are lightly browned. Pour off and discard.

Beat together the eggs, season generously and stir in the courgette and onion mixture. Melt the butter in the frying pan, add the egg mixture and cook for about 5 minutes to make a fairly firm omelette, then grill for another 3–4 minutes until lightly browned. Cut the omelette in quarters, roll up and use all 4 quarters to fill one of the canoes. Put the other canoe on top, press down firmly to seal and wrap tightly in clingfilm. Keep cool until ready to serve. Take a short knife with you to cut the *Hunter's Omelette* into 5 cm/2 in slices to be eaten at the picnic site.

Punjabi Chicken

SERVES 4–6

150 g/5 oz natural yoghurt
½ tsp crushed garlic (from a jar)
½ tsp crushed root ginger
   (from a jar) 🛒 (see page 68)
½ tsp ground cardamom 🛒 (see page 67)
½ tsp freshly ground black pepper
½ ground cumin
¼ tsp salt
4 chicken breast fillets, skinned
1 × 45 cm/18 in French stick
about 25 g/1 oz mint
juice of half a lemon

Mix half the yoghurt with the garlic, ginger, cardamom, black pepper, cumin and salt in a shallow non-metallic dish. Slash each chicken breast 4 times with a sharp knife then toss in the yoghurt mixture and leave to marinate for at least 30 minutes – up to 12 hours in the fridge is fine. Grill the chicken breasts (on a piece of foil for easy washing up) for 5–7 minutes on each side until golden brown and cooked through but not dry. Cut the French stick in half lengthwise and scoop out some of the crumb. Chop the mint leaves finely and add them to the remaining yoghurt with the lemon juice. Spread the mixture inside the split stick. When the chicken is cooked, transfer it to a carving board and, with a sharp knife, cut each breast diagonally across into 5 pieces. Put these into the lower half of the loaf, pressed reasonably closely together. Place the top half of the loaf on, press down firmly to seal and wrap tightly in clingfilm. Keep cool until ready to serve. As with the *Hunter's Omelette*, this can be sliced into 5 cm/2 in lengths to be eaten as a complete meal using your fingers at the picnic site.

Carrot Cookies

MAKES 16 BISCUITS

175 g/6 oz softened butter
75 g/3 oz caster sugar
1 egg
2 tsp grated orange rind
150 g/5 oz plain flour
100 g/4 oz porridge oats or oatmeal
2 tsp baking powder
½ tsp salt
100 g/4 oz carrot, peeled and finely grated

Preheat the oven to 190C/375F/Gas 5/170C fan (middle of the Aga roasting oven). Put all the ingredients except the carrots into a food processor and blend well. If you are making it by hand you need to cream the butter and then add the sugar and the other ingredients. Either way, add the carrots at the end and stir in thoroughly. You may need to do the next part in 2 stages. Put small tablespoonfuls of the dough onto a greased (and preferably non-stick silicone paper lined) baking tray – it should make about 16 biscuits. Leave about 4 cm/1½ in between the spoonfuls as they will spread out as they bake. Put the tray in the oven and bake for about 10–12 minutes.

Remove the cookies from the baking tray while they are still warm and leave them to cool on a wire tray where they will crisp up. They travel best if layered in kitchen paper in a rigid, airtight container.

Crafty Tips

● You can, and probably should, make this whole menu the day before. Simply pack as described in each recipe and chill the starter and main course until ready to assemble your picnic and depart.

● The *Carrot Cookies* are suitable for freezing for up to 3 months.

Wines for the great outdoors

In our climate, the rarity of being able to entertain comfortably outside instantly gives *al fresco* eating and drinking a touch of excitement and glamour. Maybe I'm just a bit childish, but for me a good picnic is one of the most hedonistic meals you could dream up. Barbecues hold rather less romance, but on a warm evening, sipping a chilled glass of wine or beer while treating your nostrils to the

charcoal thrills from the fire still holds a little magic for me.

As far as I'm concerned, the key to a good picnic or a joyous meal on the terrace has little to do with doing things classily with lots of sophistication. A folding table and chairs have always been low on the list of essentials for a picnic (no, if I'm to be entirely honest I'll admit they haven't existed on my list at all). But wine in (albeit plastic) stemmed glasses, at *the right temperature*, that's the business.

THE BIG CHILL

No matter how far from home you stray, if it's pink or it's white, it's got to be cool! Before the new age of wine chilling dawned, wet newspaper was given the job of keeping wine bottles cool. We've moved on from there now and it's more likely to be padded cylindrical bags or vacuum tubes that get the job. But remember that the wine going into these 'keep cool' containers has to be mighty cold at the start. Better, perhaps, if you're embarking on a long journey to use one of those wrap-around chillers which you freeze to numbness in the freezer first. In an emergency, if the wine just isn't cold enough when you get there, if there is water about, dangling the bottles as deeply as you can into a river or rock pool will do better than nothing, and it's worth returning them to the water until the bottle is finished.

PERFECT PICNIC WINES

Regardless of your menu, there are very few red wines designed to perform at their best on a summer's picnic. Food-and-drink matching formalities *really are* irrelevant outside. Unless you go for a very light, juicy-fruity wine such as (now sadly rare) good young Beaujolais, rosé is probably as dark a wine as you should get. Picnics are godsent for rosé wines. Sitting on a rug next to a babbling brook is no place for austere, crisp dry whites. You want something with a bit of substance and perhaps a hint of sweetness as well. Bordeaux and Bergerac are surprising sources for good rosé wines – Châteaux des Sours and Châteaux la Jaubertie to name but two.

Among white wines, the Italian Cortese grape makes gently-coddled-in-cotton-wool types, such as Gavi di Gavi, or I'd consider the silkily smooth, florally flavoured Rieslings from New Zealand or Australia.

'Food-and-drink matching formalities really are irrelevant outside.'

BEST FOR BARBECUES

In Australia, 60 per cent of all wine is bought in wine boxes. The explanation is that they live for their 'barbies' and the great outdoors. But I don't think we should follow the Ozzie lead. In Britain (and it's certainly not the same story in Australia) wine boxes tend to contain rather mediocre wine. They're also ungainly objects to chill and difficult to keep cool, a big minus if you're having a barbecue on a beach or somewhere else away from home.

In Britain, the tendency seems to be to grab for something cheap (and often not too cheerful) to drink with barbecued food. But what a mistake! There's inevitably a lot of hanging around when you cook on-the-spot and it's a perfect moment to savour an enjoyable glass or two. And the obvious choice is not necessarily red wine. Oaked white wines with big personalities complement charcoal grilling admirably, such as Spain's white Rioja Marqués de Murrietta or Australia's oaked Marsanne.

This is a picnic menu that does require plates and cutlery and stationary eating. The *Crab and Watercress Pâté* goes well on toasted breads. Two dressed Cromer crabs will give you about the right quantity of crab meat or use pre-packed frozen crab – well defrosted. Lettuce leaves are difficult to transport and on breezy days tend to fly off the plate. The *Three Bean Salad* is the solution to this. Let the beans marinate in the dressing to absorb maximum flavour before transporting them in a plastic container to the site of your picnic. The crafty way to make this salad is to use canned beans for two of the ingredients and to refresh them in cold running water before using them. With the *Hot Fruit Punch* use elderberry cordial, ideally. This is non-alcoholic but my friend, Jilly, would recommend adding a dash of liqueur (after heating) to give it that extra punch.

Crab and Watercress Pâté

SERVES 4–6

225 g/8 oz crab meat (white and brown)
2 tsp English prepared mustard
50 g/2 oz butter
2 tbsp mayonnaise (bought or see recipe page 15)
50 g/2 oz watercress, finely chopped
a little lemon juice
seasoning
dark rye crispbreads, to serve

Mix the brown crab meat with the mustard. Melt the butter and stir half of it into the white crab meat with the mayonnaise. Add the watercress to the white crab meat mixture and mix well. Check for seasoning, and you may wish to add a little lemon juice at this stage. Put half the white crab meat mixture in a 300 ml/½ pint ramekin or soufflé dish or terrine and smooth down with the back of a spoon. Mix the remaining melted butter with the brown crab meat mixture and spread that on top, then cover with the remaining white crab meat mixture to form the third layer. Smooth down. Leave in the fridge to set for at least 2 hours before removing. You can transport the pâté in a plastic container if you wish. I always leave the crispbreads in their original packing as it gives them best protection and gets them to the picnic site with the least trouble. Keep the pâté cool until ready to serve, then make sure you slice or scoop right the way down through both white and brown layers for each person. Eat it with the crispbread.

Tomato and Courgette Tarte Tatin *V*

SERVES 4–6

2 large onions
2 tbsp olive oil 🛒 (see page 15)
¼ tsp salt
1 tbsp sugar
3 tbsp water
225 g/8 oz courgettes
4 tomatoes
175 g/6 oz ready-made shortcrust pastry,
   defrosted if frozen
seasoning

Preheat the oven to 200C/400F/Gas 6/180C fan (top of the Aga roasting oven). Peel, halve and finely slice the onions. Heat the oil in a heavy-based pan and fry the onions for about 10 minutes until well softened. Stir in the salt and sugar and cook for another minute, then add the water and cook for another 3–4 minutes until reduced and tender. Spoon the onion mixture into a shallow 23 cm/9 in loose-bottomed flan tin. Trim the courgettes, cut into slices and arrange on top of the onion mixture. Cut the tomatoes into slices, discarding the stalk ends, and arrange in an overlapping layer on top of the courgettes. Season to taste.

   Roll out the pastry to a 25 cm/10 in round and place over the tomatoes, tucking the edges down the inside of the tin. Place on a baking sheet and bake for 30–35 minutes or until the pastry is golden brown. Leave until completely cool, cover with clingfilm and keep cool until needed. To serve, invert onto a flat plate and cut into slices.

Three Bean Salad *V*

SERVES 4–6

225 g/8 oz fresh green French beans
1 × 400 g/14 oz can Italian cannellini beans
1 × 400 g/14 oz can red kidney beans
1 small red or white salad onion
2 tbsp fresh lemon juice
2 tsp Dijon mustard 🛒 (see page 15)
½ tsp salt
1 tsp caster sugar
4 tbsp olive or sunflower oil
1 tbsp chopped fresh parsley

Trim the green beans, cut in half and cook for 4–5 minutes in a pan of boiling salted water. Drain and plunge into cold water to stop any further cooking. Open the cans and put the beans into a sieve. Wash thoroughly under cold running water and then leave to stand in a basin of cold water for 5 minutes. Rinse again and drain well. Peel and halve the onion and slice it very finely. Whisk together the lemon juice, mustard, salt and sugar, add the oil and whisk again. Mix the beans together, sprinkle the onion over them and then the dressing. Stir gently and sprinkle with the parsley. Pack into an airtight container and keep cool until ready to serve.

Farfalle Salmon Salad

SERVES 4–6

100 g/4 oz salmon steak
225 g/8 oz farfalle pasta (bows)
100 g/4 oz mangetout
1 tsp white wine vinegar 🛒 (see page 16)
1 tsp sugar
grated rind and juice of ½ lemon
4 tbsp olive oil 🛒 (see page 15)
2 tbsp chopped fresh herbs, such as flat-leaf
   parsley, chervil, fennel or dill
seasoning

Place the salmon in a large pan of boiling salted water and simmer gently for 5 minutes. Check if it is cooked by inserting a fork to see if the bone comes away from the flesh. Remove with a slotted spoon, drain well and divide into large flakes, discarding the bones and skin. Return the water to the boil, tip in the pasta and cook for 10–12 minutes until just tender. Drain, rinse quickly under cold running water and drain again. Meanwhile, cut the mangetout in half and place in a pan of lightly salted water. Blanch for 1 minute, drain and rinse under cold running water.

Whisk together the vinegar, sugar and lemon juice, then whisk in the oil. Stir in half the herbs and the lemon rind. Season to taste. Toss the pasta in the dressing while it is still warm. Add the salmon, mangetout and remaining herbs and toss gently to combine. Transfer to a rigid container with a lid and leave to cool completely.

Apple and Lemon Sultana Cake

SERVES 4–6

200 g/7 oz softened butter
150 g/5 oz caster sugar
225 g/8 oz self-raising flour
1½ tsp baking powder
2 large eggs
juice and grated rind of 1 lemon
1–2 tbsp milk (optional)
450 g/1 lb eating apples, peeled and cored
3 oz/75 g sultanas

Preheat the oven to 190C/375F/Gas 5/170C fan (bottom of the Aga roasting oven). If using a food processor, put all the ingredients except the apples and sultanas in and blend to a smooth paste. If you are making the cake by hand you have to use the creaming method beginning with the butter and the sugar and adding the flour, baking powder, lemon rind and juice and eggs separately. If the mixture is too stiff, add a tablespoon or two (not more) of

milk. Cut the apples into small dice and mix half of them into the cake mixture with the sultanas. Pour half the mixture into a base-lined greased 20 cm/8 in deep cake tin, add the remaining chopped apple and cover with the rest of the cake mixture. cover loosely with a piece of foil and bake in the oven for about 1 hour until risen and firm to the touch. Test with a skewer which should come out clean if the cake is cooked. If not, allow another 10 minutes or so. Cool and serve from the tin – you can just cover it with some foil to transport it. It doesn't rise to a spectacular height but is wonderfully moist.

Hot Fruit Punch

SERVES 4–6

4 whole cloves
2 substantial strips of orange peel
2 cinnamon sticks
1 tbsp soft brown sugar
750 ml/1¼ pints water
7 fl oz/200 ml elderberry or
    blackcurrant cordial
¼ pint fresh squeezed orange juice 🛒
    (see page 21)
juice of 1 lemon

Stick the cloves into the orange peel and place in a pan with the cinnamon sticks and sugar. Pour in the water, bring to the boil and simmer for 5 minutes. Add the fruit cordial, orange and lemon juice and bring just back to the boil. Pour into a warmed 1 litre/1¾ pint vacuum flask, leaving the cinnamon sticks and orange peel in the mixture. Seal the flask tightly and serve up to 4 hours later.

Crafty Tip

● As long as the crab is very fresh you can prepare this whole menu (except the punch) the day before.

HALLOWEEN

All Hallows Eve, or Halloween as it's colloquially known, precedes the day of All Saints on the 1st November. Until recently the Brits have not regarded Halloween as a cause for much celebration but in America it's always been marked. It mixes high jinks with the macabre, being the time when all the ghoulies and ghosties walk abroad before the arrival of the saints at midnight sends them back to their lairs. This has metamorphosed into hollowed-out pumpkins turned into ghostly heads with candles.

There is, however, very little tradition of special Halloween cooking in Britain. So for gastronomic precedents we really have to look to America. Here then are a couple of transatlantic recipes, plus toffee apples to give to children who might knock at the door, the tradition of 'Trick or Treat' being that the latter should be edible.

Sizzling Lamb Fajitas

SERVES 4

Fajitas come from Mexico that has no Halloween tradition at all as far as I know. But they are warming and spicy, and great to eat with your fingers.

450 g/1 lb lean lamb fillet
2 garlic cloves, peeled and crushed
1 tsp chilli powder
2 tsp sun-dried tomato purée
1 large onion
1 red pepper
1 yellow pepper
175 g/6 oz courgettes
100 g/4 oz baby sweetcorn
2 tbsp sunflower oil
seasoning
8 soft flour tortillas, soured cream, roughly chopped fresh coriander, to serve

Cut the lamb into thin slices, discarding any fat, and place in a bowl. Add the garlic, chilli powder and sun-dried tomato purée and mix well to combine. Peel, halve and slice the onion. Cut the peppers in half, remove the seeds and cut into long slices. Trim the courgettes, cut in half and then into matchsticks. Cut the sweetcorn in half lengthways. Heat the oil in a large pan and fry the lamb for 4–5 minutes until lightly browned and sealed. Add the onion, peppers, courgettes and baby sweetcorn and fry for another 3–4 minutes until the onion is just cooked through. Season to taste. Wrap the tortillas in a tea towel, put on a plate in a steamer over a pan of simmering water and warm through. To serve, place a tortilla on a serving plate and spoon over a little of the lamb mixture. Add a dollop of soured cream and a little coriander and roll up to eat.

Sizzling Lamb Fajitas

Spiced Pumpkin Pudding

SERVES 4–6

This is quite an elegant pudding with the golden colour of pumpkin and the lightness of a soufflé.

750 g/1¾ lb pumpkin, peeled and seeded
25 g/1 oz butter, melted
50 g/2 oz caster sugar
½ tsp ground allspice
½ tsp vanilla essence
2 eggs
a little icing sugar

Preheat the oven to 190C/375F/Gas 5/170C fan (middle of the Aga oven). Cut the pumpkin into cubes and poach gently in a pan of water for about 15–20 minutes until soft and easily pierced with a knife. Drain very well and purée either with a potato masher or in a food processor. Add the butter, sugar, allspice and vanilla essence, and stir until a smooth purée is formed. If it's very sloppy, allow it to dry off in a non-stick pan over a very low heat for a few minutes. Separate the eggs and stir the egg yolks into the pumpkin mixture. Beat the whites until firm and stiffened, then fold into the pumpkin mixture carefully with a large metal spoon. Put into a buttered 1.2 litre/2 pint soufflé mould or pudding dish and bake for 35–40 minutes until the pudding is risen and golden. Dust with icing sugar and serve immediately as the pudding will sink a little as it cools.

Crafty Tips

● To get ahead with the *Sizzling Lamb Fajitas*, you can prepare the lamb and mix it with the garlic, chilli powder and sun-dried tomato paste. Cover and chill for up to 24 hours. You can also chop all the vegetables and store separately in the fridge.

● The *Toffee Apples* will keep for up to a week, wrapped in clingfilm.

Toffee Apples

MAKES 8

These are old-fashioned toffee apples that you used to be able to buy at fairs and at the seaside. I have had a lifelong passion for them which I now only indulge in once a year.

8 eating apples
350 g/12 oz light muscovado sugar
50 g/2 oz butter
2 tbsp golden syrup
1 tsp red wine vinegar
120 ml/4 fl oz water

Wash the apples in mild, soapy water to remove any waxy coating, rinse well and dry. Pull off the stalks and press a 15 cm/6 in wooden skewer into the centre of each. Place the sugar, butter, golden syrup and vinegar in a heavy-based pan. Add the water and heat gently until the sugar has dissolved. Bring to the boil and boil fast until the temperature reaches 143C/290F on a sugar thermometer. Alternatively, drop a little syrup into a bowl of iced water – the syrup should form brittle threads that will snap easily between your fingers. Dip the base of the pan in cold water to prevent further cooking. Coat each apple in the syrup, and stand on a lightly oiled baking sheet or non-stick parchment paper. If the syrup hardens before all the apples are coated, heat again briefly. Once hardened, wrap each toffee apple in clingfilm.

GUY FAWKES

Guy Fawkes Night, when you are exposed to the November chill, is a great time for warming dishes, especially those that can be eaten by adults and children with equal relish. Here is a simple bean and sausage recipe that's spiced up a little bit and has sufficient variation in it to be attractive for adult palates as well, and biscuits with a combination of flavours that everybody can enjoy. The spicy fruit punch is the perfect warmer for even the coldest bonfire night and because it contains no alcohol all ages can swig it. There is hardly any work involved in creating this menu, and as the biscuits take about 50 minutes in the oven you should have the whole thing done within an hour.

Gunpowder Sausage and Bean Bake

SERVES 4–6

A lighthearted name for a delicious casserole in the French tradition. It also has some affinities with Boston Baked Beans.

1 × 400 g/14 oz can white haricot beans
1 × 400 g/14 oz can chick peas
1 onion
1 tsp sunflower oil
1 tsp crushed garlic (from a jar)
1 × 400 g/14 oz can chopped tomatoes
3 tbsp tomato purée
1 tbsp chilli sauce
1 tsp English prepared mustard
450 ml/¾ pint water
750 g/1¾ lb sausages (traditional English –
  I like beef best)
1 tbsp black treacle
2 tsp lemon juice
garlic bread, to serve

Drain the beans and chick peas and rinse them in a colander under cold running water. Drain well. Peel and finely chop the onion and fry in the oil in a large pan. Add the garlic, tomatoes, tomato purée, chilli sauce, mustard, beans and chick peas. Pour in the water, stir thoroughly and simmer gently for 20 minutes until thickened and reduced. Meanwhile, fry the sausages lightly in their own fat, drain off all the fat and bury in the bean casserole. Check for seasoning and stir in the black treacle and lemon juice. You can leave this in a low oven to keep warm while the fireworks go off. It improves in flavour for up to 1½ hours. Serve hot with garlic bread.

Dynamite Biscuits

MAKES 12

The name describes the appearance and not the taste of these biscuits. Children will love them.

225 g/8 oz softened butter
100 g/4 oz caster sugar, plus a little
  extra for dusting
225 g/8 oz plain flour
100 g/4 oz cornflour
100 g/4 oz milk chocolate
12 long pieces coconut shavings

Preheat the oven to 180C/350F/Gas 4/160C fan (bottom of the Aga roasting oven). Place the butter, sugar, flour and cornflour in a food processor and blend until smooth and the mixture binds together. You could do this by the traditional method of creaming together the butter and sugar until soft and fluffy, adding the flour and stirring until the mixture binds together. Turn out on to a lightly floured board and knead lightly until smooth. Press into a 20 cm/8 in square, lightly buttered baking tin. Prick well with a fork and bake for 45–50 minutes or until golden brown and cooked through. Leave for 5 minutes, then cut into twelve fingers and transfer to a wire tray to cool. Meanwhile, break the chocolate into pieces and melt in a heatproof bowl over a pan of hot water. Dip one end of each biscuit into the chocolate and stick in a piece of coconut to make a 'fuse'. Place on a piece of non-stick silicone paper and leave to set completely, then transfer to an airtight container until ready to serve.

Crafty Tip

● You can make the *Gunpowder Sausage and Bean Bake* and *Dynamite Biscuits* up to 24 hours in advance. Cover the casserole and chill until ready to reheat and serve. Store the biscuits in an airtight container until ready to serve.

Spiced Fruit Punch

SERVES 4–6

Guy Fawkes Night is one of those celebrations when children are at the heart of the event. This is a punch that parents and children will enjoy equally.

1 orange
8 whole cloves
2 red-skinned eating apples
1 cinnamon stick
2 tbsp light muscovado sugar
1 bottle Duchy Originals red fruit and herb
  blend 🛒 or 750 ml/1¼ pints of sparkling
  red grape juice

Cut the orange into slices, discarding the ends, then cut each slice in half. Push one clove into 8 of the slices. Remove the cores from the apples and cut into wedges. Place the orange slices in a pan with the apple, cinnamon stick and sugar and pour in the Duchy Originals or red grape juice. Heat through gently, stirring occasionally, until the sugar has dissolved. Regulate the heat to ensure the liquid does not boil. Serve the punch in heat-resistant glasses with some orange and apple slices.

DUCHY ORIGINALS
Duchy Originals are new, refreshing, lightly sparkling, non-alcoholic red and white herb and fruit blends which are on sale in selected stores and delicatessens. The fruit comes from the National Fruit Collection at Brogdale, Kent, and selected English growers. Duchy Originals Limited was set up by the Prince of Wales in 1990 as an independent company to develop quality products for home and export markets. As an alternative, use sparkling red grape juice.

THANKSGIVING

Thanksgiving is a special day in America to commemorate the first year the Pilgrim Fathers survived after they'd landed in Massachusetts. As well as being a public holiday it's a day full of special celebrations. Children help to make the food, and the food itself is almost exclusively made from ingredients that the settlers found when they arrived. The central dish is roast turkey. With it are eaten mashed potatoes, candied sweet potatoes, cornbread, a variety of relishes based on cranberries and a stuffing. The meal is usually finished with pecan pie, served with a scoop of ice-cream or a dollop of whipped cream. You'll be relieved to know that 3 hours, not all of it working, should be enough to put a spectacular meal on the table.

Thanksgiving Roast Turkey with Gravy

When you're roasting a turkey, if it's been frozen or chilled make sure it's fully up to room temperature before you start. The bigger the turkey the less minutes per 450 g/1 lb you need to cook it for. A rough guide is:
4.5–5.5 kg/10–12 lb turkey needs about 17–18 minutes per 450 g/1 lb
7–8 kg/15–18 lb turkey needs about 15 minutes per 450 g/1 lb
9 kg/20 lb plus turkey needs about 12 minutes per 450 g/1 lb.

If you have a frozen turkey it is essential that it is thawed in a cool place, and that sufficient time is allowed for this. A small bird will take up to 18 hours and a large bird 36 hours.

1 turkey, with giblets
2 onions
1 bay leaf
750 ml/1¼ pints water
salt

Preheat the oven to 190C/375F/Gas 4/170C fan (bottom of the Aga roasting oven). Weigh the turkey, place it on a rack and put a peeled, halved onion inside. Cover it with butter papers or buttered foil, particularly around the legs and thighs, and roast for the calculated length of time (see times above), uncovering it for the last 45 minutes or so to allow the turkey to go golden brown all over.

Meanwhile, put all the giblets (except for the liver) into a pan with the bay leaf, the water, a roughly chopped onion and a good pinch of salt and simmer for about 1–1½ hours. When you have achieved a well-flavoured stock, strain and set aside. When the turkey is cooked and the juices run clear from the thigh, transfer it to a large carving plate to stand for about 15–20 minutes. Pour the stock into the roasting tin and bring quickly to the boil, scraping down the bottom of the tin. Use this to make the gravy (see page 184).

FAR LEFT
Pecan Pie
(see page 186)

BELOW LEFT
Candied Sweet Potatoes
(see page 185)

and Cranberry Relish
(see page 185)

MIDDLE
Thanksgiving Roast Turkey with
Gravy
(see page 181)

TOP
Cornbread
(see page 186)

BELOW
Vermont Style Stuffing
(see page 184)

For the gravy:
40 g/1½ oz butter
40 g/1½ oz plain flour
120 ml/4 fl oz single cream
seasoning

Melt the butter in a non-stick pan, remove from the heat and stir in the flour. Return to the pan and cook over a medium heat until golden brown, stirring continuously. Pour in the reserved giblet stock from the roasting tin a little at a time, whisking thoroughly after each addition until smooth. Bring to the boil, stir in the cream, season generously and remove from the heat. Pour into a gravy boat to serve. Slice the turkey in the conventional way and serve with the gravy, *Vermont Style Stuffing*, *Cranberry Relish*, conventional mashed potatoes, *Candied Sweet Potatoes* and hot buttered broccoli.

Vermont Style Stuffing

SERVES 6–8

Every part of America has its own style of stuffing. In Florida it will contain citrus flavours, in New Mexico chilli, in the Mid West sweetcorn, apples in Oregon and cornbread in Louisiana. This recipe, which comes from Vermont, is perhaps closer to our traditions.

225 g/8 oz dried chestnuts, soaked, or
  450 g/1 lb vacuum-packed chestnuts or
  fresh chestnuts, peeled 🛒
450 ml/¾ pint chicken stock
225 g/8 oz white bread with crusts removed
100 g/4 oz butter
100 g/4 oz onion, peeled and finely chopped
100 g/4 oz celery, finely chopped
2 tsp chopped fresh tarragon or ½ tsp freeze-
  dried tarragon 🛒 **(see page 53)**
2 tsp chopped fresh sage or ½ tsp freeze-
  dried sage 🛒 **(see page 53)**
1 tsp salt
½ tsp freshly ground black pepper
1 large egg

Whether using soaked, dried chestnuts, fresh or ready-peeled vacuum-packed ones, put them into the chicken stock and simmer gently for about 30 minutes until they are cooked through and tender but not mushy. Remove the chestnuts with a slotted spoon and roughly crumble or finely chop. Cut the bread into 1 cm/½ in cubes, put into a large bowl and pour over the chicken stock. Melt the butter in a frying pan and gently fry the onion and celery until softened. Add to the bread mixture with the chestnuts, herbs, salt and pepper and stir in the egg. You can use this to stuff the turkey or place in a gratin or small roasting tin at least 25 cm/1 in deep and baked in the same oven, 180C/350F/Gas 4/160C fan (bottom of the Aga roasting oven), for the last hour that the turkey is cooking. If you do it this way I find it helps to put a couple of butter papers over the stuffing as well as the turkey for the first 30 minutes. They help to produce a lovely, crispy-topped, moist and succulent stuffing to serve with the roast turkey.

CHESTNUTS
You can buy ready-peeled chestnuts in cans or long-life vacuum packs. They are certainly a much craftier option than peeling your own, but dried chestnuts soaked for an hour in boiling water are excellent too. To peel fresh ones, slit along one side with a knife, boil for 2 minutes and take the skins off, keeping the remaining chestnuts waiting warm in the water.

Cranberry Relish (V)

SERVES 6–8

The tradition of mixing cranberries with citrus fruits goes back a long way in New England. I can remember at a family Thanksgiving some years ago a fresh relish made from a mixture of finely chopped walnuts, whole oranges and cranberries for which there was no cooking involved at all. This one uses three different citrus fruits to produce a vividly flavoured cranberry preserve to eat with the turkey.

half a lemon, pips removed and peeled
half an orange, pips removed and peeled
half a lime, pips removed and peeled
450 g/1 lb fresh or frozen whole cranberries
100 g/4 oz sugar
pinch of ground cinnamon
pinch of ground nutmeg

Cut the lemon, orange and lime flesh into small pieces and place in a food processor with the cranberries and process for 30 seconds or so until the mixture is finely minced and ground up. Transfer to a non-stick pan and add the sugar, stirring thoroughly to combine before heating gently. When it comes to the boil, add the spices and simmer for about 30 minutes until the mixture has thickened and reduced by about a quarter. Make sure it doesn't burn. You may need to add 1–2 tablespoons of water if the citrus fruits were not very juicy. Allow to cool. If you want to keep some of it you have to pot it hot as though it was a jam, sealing the lids down. It will keep for up to 3 months. Put some into two small bowls to serve.

Candied Sweet Potatoes (V)

SERVES 6–8

The other unusual Thanksgiving dish which is a must for most Americans is *Candied Sweet Potatoes*, also known in parts of America as Louisiana yams. Sweet potatoes, an indigenous American vegetable, are eaten in a lot of different ways and absolutely scrumptious baked and eaten with butter and salt like ordinary potatoes. However, at Thanksgiving they are given special treatment. In Britain you can buy them all year round and they come in two varieties, white and golden. I prefer the golden ones although there is a view that the white one is the connoisseurs' variety.

1 kg/2 lb sweet potatoes
grated rind and juice of 1 tangerine
4 tbsp soft brown sugar
50 g/2 oz butter plus extra for greasing
½ tsp ground allspice

Scrub and trim the sweet potatoes and put them to boil in salted water. They cook rather quicker than conventional potatoes so, depending on their size, about 10 minutes is probably right. Drain and skin them – the skin will just slip off. Slice them into 2.5 cm/1 in thick rounds and arrange in overlapping layers in a lightly buttered gratin dish. Mix together the tangerine rind, juice and sugar and drizzle evenly over the sweet potatoes. Dot with the butter and sprinkle over the allspice. This can be done a little bit in advance but do not refrigerate. About 15 minutes before serving, put the sweet potatoes under a pre-heated grill and allow the surface to caramelise and go golden, and almost singed, brown. Serve at once bubbling in the dish.

Cornbread Ⓥ

SERVES 6–8

This American dish and is a lovely, light, golden breakfast or speciality bread, perhaps more like the French brioche than a conventional loaf. It is also eaten warm sometimes at breakfast, particularly in the New Orleans area, with a mixture of soft scrambled eggs, red and green peppers and onions. I like to leave this golden bread to get cold, then have it toasted with cheese when it is scrumptious.

400 g/14 oz strong plain flour
275 g/10 oz medium yellow corn meal
   (ground yellow maize NOT cornflour!)
2 tbsp sugar
2 tbsp baking powder
1 tsp salt
2 eggs
225 ml/8 fl oz milk
4 tbsp sunflower or soya oil plus extra for
   greasing
2 tbsp natural yoghurt

Preheat the oven to 190C/375F/Gas 5/170C fan (middle of the Aga roasting oven). Grease a 1 kg/ 2 lb loaf tin, even if it is non-stick. Put the flour, cornmeal, sugar, baking powder and salt into a bowl, and beat in the eggs. Add the milk, oil and yoghurt. You can mix all the liquids together first if you like, then just pour the lot in. Give it a really good stir until the dough comes together. Turn out on to a lightly floured surface and knead the dough for a few minutes until smooth. Smooth down and shape into the prepared loaf tin. Bake for 55 minutes and test it with a skewer. If it comes out smeared, it needs another 5 minutes, but turn the oven off. When it is ready, take the bread out, let it stand for 5 minutes, then turn it out. You may find sliding a knife round the edge will help. Let it cool for a minute or two before serving it sliced with the rest of the Thanksgiving meal.

Pecan Pie

SERVES 6–8

225 g/8 oz digestive biscuits
75 g/3 oz unsalted butter, melted
50 g/2 oz light brown sugar

For the filling:
100 g/4 oz unsalted butter
175 g/6 oz golden syrup
2 eggs, lightly beaten
100 g/4 oz pecan nut halves
ice-cream 🛒 (see page 41) or whipped cream,
   to serve

Preheat the oven to 180C/350F/Gas 6/160C fan (top of the Aga roasting oven). Put the biscuits into a food processor and process until the mixture resembles fine breadcrumbs. Add the butter and sugar and mix thoroughly. Use to line the bottom and sides of a 20 cm/10 in loose-bottomed flan tin. Bake for 20 minutes until set.

   Meanwhile, make the filling. Place the butter, syrup and eggs in a non-stick pan and stir until melted and well combined. Remove from the heat. Reserve nine of the best pecan nut halves for decoration and put the remainder in the food processor and whizz for 10 seconds until roughly chopped. Stir into the syrup mixture and pour into the prepared biscuit base. Return to the oven and bake for another 25–30 minutes until risen and just set. Arrange the reserved pecan nut halves on top and bake for another 5–10 minutes until golden brown. This is wonderful with ice-cream or cream.

Crafty Tips

● You can prepare the *Vermont Style Stuffing* ready to bake and the cooked *Cranberry Relish*, *Cornbread* and *Pecan Pie* up to 12 hours ahead.

● The *Pecan Pie* will freeze for up to 3 months.

CELEBRATIONS

Perhaps the most difficult kind of entertaining to organise is when big numbers are involved. When a dinner party changes from four to fourteen people, or you're suddenly presented with a whole gang of ravenous teenagers, even the most experienced of cooks can panic. What one needs is some forward planning and simple but exciting dishes.

Once again, all the dishes here are designed to be prepared in advance. So, for a celebration birthday lunch for family and friends, or a wedding party for 50 or more, entertaining in large numbers has never been so easy. You might even enjoy the occasion yourself!

ENTERTAINING 8–10 TEENAGERS

Teenagers can be quite difficult to cook for, especially in large numbers. Their taste for fast food is indisputable but, nowadays, there are other strong influences too. Firstly there is the vegetarian trend. Then there's the issue of slimming and/or health which makes salads popular. And last, but not least, the dictates of food fashion are increasingly significant, with Italian-style foods, pizzas and pastas rating very high on most score sheets.

This menu should be achievable in just about 1 hour. However, most of the dishes can be prepared well in advance allowing a much easier time for you. Teenagers don't need much of an excuse for a party, whether it be someone's birthday, the passing of a driving test or even an exam.

Crispy Potato Skins with Salsa and Soured Cream (V)

SERVES 8–10

A home-made version of one of the great American fast food favourites.

12 × 100 g/4 oz potatoes
5 tbsp sunflower oil
450 g/1 lb ripe tomatoes
6 spring onions
1 green chilli
3 tbsp chilli sauce
150 ml/¼ pint soured cream
2 tbsp snipped fresh chives
1 small garlic clove, peeled and crushed (optional)
seasoning

Preheat the oven to 200C/400F/Gas 6/180C fan (top of the Aga roasting oven). Scrub the potatoes and dry them well with paper towels. Rub the potatoes with 3 tablespoons of the oil and place them directly on the oven shelf. Bake for 40–45 minutes or until the potatoes are slightly softened when squeezed.

Meanwhile make the dips. For the salsa, chop the tomatoes, spring onions and chilli, mix with the chilli sauce and season to taste. In another bowl, mix together the soured cream, chives and garlic, if using, and season to taste. Place the salsa in three small bowls or ramekins and the soured cream in another. Cover the dips and chill.

When the potatoes are tender, remove them from the oven and cut them in half lengthways and then into quarters. Slice away, and discard, a bit of the flesh, leaving a layer of potato at least 1 cm/½ in thick from the skin. Arrange the potato skins on baking sheets skin side up, brush with the remaining oil and grill for 5–10 minutes until crisp and golden brown. Arrange the potato skins on serving plates with the dips, sprinkle with a little salt and serve hot.

Tuna Pasta Pie

SERVES 8-10

This is a storecupboard favourite which needs to be made in sufficiently large quantities to cope with the inevitable second helpings. It is also a one- pot dish which has at least the advantage of controlling the washing up.

1.2 litres/2 pints milk
50 g/2 oz butter
50 g/2 oz plain flour
1 tsp ground bay leaves
1 tbsp English mustard, prepared
75 g/3 oz freshly grated Parmesan cheese
675 g/1½ lb small pasta shapes (quills,
**   spirals, ears, little hats, etc.)** 🛒
**   (see page 18)**
3 × 400 g/14 oz cans tuna in oil
1kg/2 lb mixed frozen vegetables,
**   such as broccoli and cauliflower**
**   florets and sliced carrots**
seasoning

Preheat the oven to 200C/400F/Gas 6/180C fan (top of the Aga roasting oven). Whisk together the milk, butter and flour in a pan and bring gently to the boil, whisking occasionally. When the sauce is smooth and thick, add the ground bay leaves and mustard, stir well and simmer for 2–3 minutes. Stir in 50 g/2 oz of the Parmesan and remove from the heat. Cook the pasta in a large pan of boiling salted water for 3–4 minutes. Remove from the heat and leave to stand for another 8–10 minutes with the lid on and then drain. Open the cans of tuna and drain them well – they should give you 750 g/1¾ lb of tuna in total.

Mix a third of the white sauce into the warm drained pasta and set aside. Put the frozen vegetables into a pan of boiling salted water and cook according to the instructions on the packet until just tender. Drain and add to the remaining white sauce with the tuna. Mix together with a large metal spoon until well combined and check for

seasoning – it may need a little salt or pepper. Place in a 5 litre/9 pint pie or soufflé dish. Spread the pasta mixture on top and sprinkle with the remaining Parmesan. Bake for 25–30 minutes until the top is lightly golden and bubbling – this may take a little longer if you have allowed the dish to cool completely first.

Pizza Margherita

SERVES 8-10

Pizzas originated in Naples and if you've been to Italy on holiday, you'll know how wonderful the real thing is. They are simple to make, especially if you buy pizza bases from the supermarkets which sell all kinds of shapes and sizes, or you could always use a French stick. The colours of this most traditional of pizza toppings are green, white and red – the colours of the Italian flag. However, you can experiment with different toppings.

2 ready-made 20 cm/8 in pizza bases
2 tbsp tomato purée
1 × 200 g/7 oz can Italian chopped tomatoes
225 g/8 oz Mozzarella, thinly sliced
100 g/4 oz freshly grated Parmesan
1 tbsp chopped fresh basil
1 tbsp chopped fresh oregano
seasoning
2 tsp olive oil 🛒 **(see page 15)**

Preheat the oven to 220C/425F/Gas 7/200C fan (top of the Aga roasting oven). Preheat two baking sheets. Spread one tablespoon of the tomato purée over each pizza base, making sure it reaches the edges. Spoon over the chopped tomatoes and spread them evenly as well. Lay the Mozzarella slices on top and sprinkle over the Parmesan and herbs and season generously. Add any toppings you like at this stage, then drizzle over the olive oil. Place a pizza on each preheated baking sheet and bake for 10–15 minutes until bubbling and golden.

LEFT
Crispy Potato Skins with Salsa and Soured Cream
(see page 188)

BELOW LEFT
Spiced Fruit Parcels
(see page 192)

BELOW
Tuna Pasta Pie
(see page 189)

Californian Layered Salad Ⓥ

SERVES 8-10

Californian salad is a mixture of fruit, salad vegetables and low fat cottage cheese. As with all layered salads the combination should look attractive as well as taste good. You can layer this up in a glass bowl, or use any plastic bowl that is the correct size and turn out for a spectacular effect.

1 medium-sized melon
1 large mango
1 red pepper
2 little gem lettuces, washed
225 g/8 oz strawberries
4 tbsp sunflower oil
2 tbsp lemon juice
½ tsp salt
½ tsp sugar
1 tsp wholegrain mustard
225 g/8 oz low fat cottage cheese
   with pineapple
175 g/6 oz beansprouts

Cut the melon into four and remove the seeds. Cut each quarter away from the peel and cut into 1 cm/½ in pieces. Cut the cheeks off the mango, halve each cheek, remove the peel and cut into 1 cm/½in pieces. Cut the top off the red pepper, remove the seeds and cut into rings. Slice the little gem lettuces across the grain into 5 mm/¼ in ribbons. Hull the strawberries and cut into slices. Put the oil, lemon juice, salt, sugar and mustard in a screw-topped jar and shake together until well mixed. Place the red pepper rings in the bottom of a 3.5 litre/6 pint bowl and put the melon on top. Spoon over a layer of cottage cheese and arrange the sliced strawberries and mango on top. Next put in the beansprouts and finish with the shredded lettuce. Drizzle over the dressing. You can chill this salad for up to 30 minutes before serving. If not servingd from the bowl, invert on to a plate and show off the layers.

Spiced Fruit Parcels

SERVES 10

This recipe will get your teenagers to eat fruit without realising that it might do them good.

250 ml/8 fl oz freshly squeezed orange
   juice 🛒 (see page 21)
8 tbsp lime marmalade
8 bananas
675 g/1½ lb strawberries
100 g/4 oz toasted flaked almonds
vanilla ice-cream, to serve 🛒 (see page 41)

Preheat the oven to 200C/400F/Gas 6/180C fan (top of the Aga roasting oven). Heat the orange juice and lime marmalade in a small pan, stirring, until the marmalade has melted. Remove from the heat and allow to cool. Peel the bananas and cut into 1 cm/½ in slices. Hull the strawberries and cut each one in half. Cut out 10 × 25 cm/10 in squares of aluminium foil and divide the fruit among them. Turn up the edges of the foil to catch the liquid and drizzle over the orange and lime marmalade mixture. Bring up the edges together to seal the parcels, making sure you leave plenty of room for air. Place on a large baking sheet and bake for 10–15 minutes. Open each parcel, sprinkle over a few almonds and serve with a scoop of ice-cream.

Crafty Tips

● Almost the entire menu can be prepared the day before except the salad which shouldn't sit for more than 2 hours or the lettuce will begin to wilt.

● The *Tuna Pasta Pie* needs to be left to cool completely then covered and chilled.

● The *Spiced Fruit Parcels* can be left in their foil wrappers in the fridge.

Californian Layered Salad

Party wines

'. . . better to go for a standard bottle which is in any event easier to chill and cheaper to try out before the event.'

'Never mind the quality, feel the width' used to be the maxim for party wine buying. For some reason it was presumed that party goers left their tastebuds behind. But during a lull in conversation, or having your ear bent by a total bore, your thoughts can easily focus on the wine in your glass, and deciding it is barely drinkable doesn't really help to put you in the party swing.

Wine shops used to have 'party' sections stacked with cheap and frankly not very cheerful wines dressed up in enormous bottles. Certainly there *is* a saving to be had on large sizes, but regrettably you seldom find a wine in a big bottle you want to drink at length. My advice: steer clear of them. Likewise wine boxes. You pay a premium price on a wine box for the technology designed to keep opened wine fresh for a couple of months. There is little point in blowing the 'technology' (and the extra expense) in a single evening. No, better to go for a standard bottle which is in any event easier to chill and cheaper to try out before the event.

WHAT TO BUY

Having said you certainly don't want rubbish, it isn't necessary to buy very expensive wine for a big party either. Ideally you want easy-drinking wines with a bit of personality, where whites are concerned, not lean and mean. Chardonnay springs to mind – and there's plenty of choice on the wine shop shelves at a wide range of prices. Pinot Noir is a friendly red grape (although it can be expensive), or go for a New World Cabernet Sauvignon, particularly from Chile. If you decide on sparkling wine instead, you'll find recommendations on page 216. If your budget is very tight, go for an inexpensive, dry white wine – or sparkling wine – and make it into an exotic Kir with crème de cassis or crème de mûre. These are fruit-based liqueurs – blackcurrant and blackberry respectively. A tiny dash in the bottom of the glass before you pour in the wine or fizz dyes it a tender pink and gives the wine all the fruit and friendliness you could ask for – plus a heady aroma, too. Less expensive are the 'sirops' made from the same fruits, but without alcohol – but remember a bottle of the actual liqueur will be plenty for even a big party (so long as you only use a few drops at a time).

WHERE TO BUY

	Advantages	Disadvantages
SUPERMARKET	• Good range • Good prices • Familiar with wines on sale • Multibuy deals sometimes available	• No sale or return • Seldom glass loan • No delivery • Seldom case discount
HIGH STREET WINE CHAIN	• Sale or return • Glass loan • Case discount • Free local delivery • Sometimes party planning service on offer	• Pricier than supermarkets • Sometimes poorer range
WINE MERCHANT	• Good advice and service • Glass loan • Delivery	• More expensive • Limited choice of inexpensive wines
CROSS CHANNEL SHOPPING	• Cheapest wine (but take account of your fare) • Exciting shopping • There may be a branch of your favourite supermarket across the Channel	• Beware! possible poor quality • More difficult to try before you buy • No sale or return • No glass loan • No delivery • No New World wines

• Individual outlets in several of these categories may sell ice – look out for it when you shop because you'll need quantities of ice to chill your wine.

ADDITIONAL INFORMATION ABOUT CROSS CHANNEL SHOPPING

There is no limit to the amount of wine you can bring into Britain from other countries in the EC so long as it is purely for personal use. If you cross the Channel and buy in a French supermarket or from an unfamiliar trader, all that tempts may not be delicious. There is a lot of poor wine made in France. Little of it is imported into Britain because there isn't much point in importing rubbish and paying our high taxes on it, *but* lots of it is for sale at cheap prices on the other side of the Channel. Never buy quantities of a wine you haven't tried, so before you embark on your journey equip yourself with some glasses and a corkscrew. When you get there, select a few possible wines from the shop shelves and buy a single bottle of each one, take them back to your car, open them up and try them, attempting to be as objective as you can. Remember, you're likely to be much more critical when you finally serve them at home, so go on trying out wines until you find some you definitely like. Only then buy the quantities you require. Even if you're buying Champagne, try a bottle first because there can be some pretty disappointing bottles out there. It may be worth getting in stocks of mineral water while you're about it. And beer. There are some very good beer buys to be had, but either try before you buy, or go for a brand you know.

'A tiny dash in the bottom of the glass before you pour in the wine or fizz ... gives the wine all the fruit and friendliness you could ask for ...'

ESSENTIAL PARTY-GIVING POINTS TO REMEMBER

Make sure all white wines, beers and soft drinks are thoroughly chilled. You should be able to buy ice in bulk locally – even if you can't find it in a wine shop, ask in off-licences, garages or your local fishmonger to order some in for you. You then need a large receptacle for ice and bottles – clean buckets or a scrubbed dustbin will do, as will the bath. A word of warning here: If you have bought your wine on sale or return, chill on ice only the bottles you are sure you'll use. Your reserve wines should be chilled in a fridge, because if the labels float off in the icy water, the shop won't take them back.

Make sure the glasses are scrupulously clean – borrowed or hired glasses seldom arrive as clean as you would want.

Always offer plenty of soft drink alternatives. If your guests don't want the alcoholic drink on offer, they may not simply want mineral water or orange juice instead. There are plenty of interesting soft drinks around, or you could make your own fruit cup (see recipe page 80).

If you decide to offer an alcoholic punch or cup, write a recipe card and display it by the punchbowl so your guests know what they're in for. Not only will they like to know what they're getting, but they will also want to know how alcoholic the drink is, so they can pace themselves.

If you are giving a 'drinks' party, it's important to offer some sort of food – even if it is only in the shape of twiglets and crisps. For a more elaborate approach see Michael's canapés (page 112–14). It's important to have sufficient 'pourers' on hand to top up drinks. You may be too busy to manage the whole room by yourself.

Cream of Salmon Soup

SERVES 8–10

**675 g/1½ lb salmon, filleted and skinned,
   plus some trimmings (ask your fishmonger
   or fish counter for about 675 g/1½ lb,
   or use fish stock)
2.5 litres/4½ pints water
2 bay leaves
50 ml/2 fl oz white wine vinegar** 🛒
   **(see page 16)
1 onion, peeled, halved, stuck with 2 cloves
half a lemon
1 tsp salt
10 peppercorns
300 ml/½ pint double cream
2 egg yolks
2 tbsp cornflour
freshly ground black pepper
chopped fresh dill or chives, to garnish**

Put the salmon trimmings, skin, bones, and any
other bits that your fishmonger has donated, into
a large pan with the water, bay leaves, wine vinegar,
onion, lemon, salt and peppercorns. Bring to the
boil and simmer gently for 20 minutes. Strain,
discard all the bits and return to the pan. Cut the
piece of salmon into 1 cm/½ in cubes and poach
gently in the stock for about 5 minutes until firm
but not at all flaky. Remove carefully with a slotted
spoon, reserve a third and process the rest in a food
processor with a couple of tablespoons of the stock.
Mix together the cream, egg yolks and cornflour
thoroughly in a bowl and add a ladleful of the hot
stock. Stir round until well blended and tip the
mixture into the pan. Stir thoroughly and bring to
the boil very gently, turning the heat off as soon as
the mixture begins to bubble. It will thicken and go
very creamy. Add the minced salmon mixture and
ladle into soup bowls. Garnish with the reserved
salmon and serve immediately. You can sprinkle
this soup with a little green – dill or chives – and
some freshly ground black pepper.

ENTERTAINING
8–10
ADULTS

Special occasion entertaining for
adults can be a problem. Getting
the balance right, for both pleasure
and waistline, is often a matter of
fine judgement. What I suggest here
is a refined but simple soup with the
luxurious flavour of salmon, needing
nothing more than a sprinkling of
dill or chives to garnish. The main
course is a new twist on that old
favourite, lasagne. The focaccia offers
the perfect accompaniment so that
this course needs nothing more than
a simply dressed green salad. And
for the pudding I have chosen an
unusual way of cooking a fruit tart.

It should take no more than an
hour in all. But the main course does
display some care and an element of
crafty skill to demonstrate that extra
trouble *has* been taken.

Lasagnette Tricolore

SERVES 8–10

Lasagnette is a new form of pasta, at least new to Britain. It comes in long, quite wide (2.5 cm/1 in) strips with slightly frilly edges. In this dish it's used in a similar way to its elder relative, lasagne. It's easier to handle and much more interesting to look at and to eat. If you'd like a vegetarian version of the dish, you can leave out the chicken liver, in which case I would suggest adding 225 g/8 oz of Florentine-style fennel cut into 1 cm/½ in thick slices and cooked in the same way. This dish has three simple stages to it building up into a complex, delicious, layered confection.

400 g/14 oz lasagnette
2 tbsp olive oil 🛒 (see page 15)
25 g/1 oz butter
675 g/1½ lb chicken livers, defrosted if
    frozen, washed and drained
1 large onion, peeled and finely chopped
2 garlic cloves, peeled and finely chopped
seasoning
225 g/8 oz mushrooms, sliced
1 × 400 g/14 oz can chopped tomatoes
4 tbsp tomato purée
6 tbsp crème fraîche 🛒 (see page 58) or
    double cream
2 tbsp chopped fresh parsley

For the spinach sauce:
50 g/2 oz butter
75 g/3 oz plain flour
750 ml/1¼ pints of milk
seasoning
½ tsp freshly grated nutmeg
675 g/1½ lb fresh spinach leaves, washed
    and trimmed, or 350 g/12 oz frozen
    spinach, defrosted and squeezed dry
75 g/3 oz freshly grated Parmesan cheese
Hot Tapenade Focaccia (see recipe page 200),
    and green salad, to serve

Cook the pasta in a large pan of boiling salted water for 3 minutes, then take off the heat and set aside with the lid on for 7–8 minutes until the pasta is tender and cooked through. Drain well. Meanwhile, heat the oil and butter in a large frying pan and add the chicken livers, onion, garlic and seasoning and fry until the onion has softened. Add the mushrooms and fry for another 5 minutes. Stir in the chopped tomatoes, tomato purée, crème fraîche or cream and parsley. Simmer for 5–10 minutes until reduced and thickened slightly. Season to taste and set aside.

Put the butter, flour and milk in a non-stick pan, heat gently and whisk together until smooth and thickened. Season generously then add the nutmeg. Simmer for 2–3 minutes. If using frozen spinach, add this to the sauce at this point and heat gently. If you're using fresh spinach, place in a large pan of boiling water and cook for 2–3 minutes until softened. Drain well and squeeze out all the excess water. Leave to cool a little, then finely chop and stir into the sauce. Add 50 g/2 oz of the Parmesan to the sauce.

Put one-third of the pasta strips into the bottom of a 25 cm × 30 cm/10 × 12 in deep roasting tin or 5 litre/9 pint ovenproof dish. Spoon over half the chicken liver mixture and arrange another layer of lasagnette on top. Pour over the remaining chicken liver sauce, then top with the rest of the lasagnette. Spoon over the spinach sauce to cover the lasagnette. Scatter over the remaining Parmesan and grill until lightly golden and bubbling. Serve hot, cut into portions as part of the buffet.

Lasagnette Tricolore

Hot Tapenade Focaccia

SERVES 8-10

This is an outrageous mixture of French and Italian flavours. Because of their developing in neighbouring regions, they go superbly together.

75 g/3 oz softened butter
2 garlic cloves, peeled and chopped
4 tbsp green olive tapenade (available in supermarkets or delicatessens)
2 focaccia

Preheat the oven to 200C/400F/Gas 6/180C fan (top of the Aga roasting oven). Place the butter, garlic and tapenade in a food processor or liquidiser and whizz until blended. Cut each focaccia in half horizontally and divide the butter mixture between the halves. Spread to the edges using a round-bladed knife and sandwich the halves back together. Wrap the focaccia in a sheet of aluminium foil and bake in the oven for 15–20 minutes until piping hot and slightly crispy. Remove the foil, cut each focaccia into eight wedges and serve hot.

Apricot Upside-down Tart

SERVES 8-10

Upside-down tarts are classically made with apples but I have found they go equally well with apricots.

14 apricots or 2 × 400 g/14 oz cans apricot halves in natural juice
75 g/3 oz butter
75 g/3 oz sugar
2 tbsp double cream
1 tsp ground cinnamon
350 g/12 oz ready-made puff pastry, defrosted if frozen 🛒 (see page 142)
whipped cream, to serve

Preheat the oven to 200C/400F/Gas 6/180C fan (top of the Aga roasting oven). If using fresh apricots, plunge them in a pan of boiling water for 1 minute. Remove with a slotted spoon and plunge into cold water. Peel away the skins, cut in halves and remove the stones. Melt the butter and sugar in a small pan. Bring to the boil and simmer for 3–4 minutes, beating continuously until thickened and smooth. Remove from the heat, leave to cool for 1 minute, then stir in the cream and cinnamon. Pour into a shallow 30 cm/12 in flan tin and arrange the fresh or canned apricots on top, cut side up. Roll out the pastry to a 33 cm/13 in round. Place over the apricots, pushing the edges down the insides of the tin, trimming off any excess pastry. Prick all over with a fork and place on a baking sheet. Bake for 25–30 minutes or until the pastry is risen and golden brown. Loosen the pastry from the edges of the tin with a palette knife and leave for 5 minutes. Invert on to a heatproof plate and grill for 3–4 minutes until bubbling and caramelised. Serve each slice with a dollop of whipped cream.

Crafty Tips

● This menu can be prepared the day before, allowing you no last minute worries on the day of your party. Simply cover each dish with clingfilm and chill.

● The *Cream of Salmon Soup* will just need to be reheated, while the *Lasagnette Tricolore* will need to be baked in a preheated oven, 200C/400F/Gas 6/180C fan (top of the Aga roasting oven), for 30–40 minutes until heated through and the top is lightly golden.

● The *Hot Tapenade Focaccia* and *Apricot Upside-down Tart* can just be baked as described in the recipes.

● All the dishes on this menu are suitable for freezing for up to 3 months.

Apricot Upside-down Tart

ENTERTAINING 14–16 PEOPLE

This menu has been designed so that it could be served either as a hot buffet or as a seated affair, providing you have enough table, space and chairs! The first and last courses can be prepared well in advance and set aside ready to serve with just a few last minute things to do. The sauce for the main course, *Seafood Feuilletté*, will sit quietly keeping warm over a low heat or in a warming oven without any trouble for an hour or so. It does require just a little last minute preparation but there's the consolation that it is spectacular. Bowls of the *Lemon and Almond Rice* can also be prepared ahead and left in the fridge until needed.

Layered Chicken Terrine

MAKES 16 SLICES

One of the prettiest and visually most complex dishes to present to your guests. It is, however, simplicity itself.

675 g/1½ lb boneless chicken pieces
3 eggs
freshly ground black pepper
1 tbsp lemon juice
2 tbsp chopped fresh tarragon
2 tbsp chopped fresh parsley
450 ml/¾ pint double cream
salt
25 g/1 oz butter
225 g/8 oz French beans
175 g/6 oz baby carrots
1 tbsp green peppercorns

For the tomato sauce:
600 ml/1 pint *famiglia sugo* or *sugo casa* 🛒 (see page 19)
2 tbsp chopped fresh herbs, such as basil or chervil
pinch of sugar
seasoning

Preheat the oven to 180C/350F/Gas 4/160C fan (middle of the Aga roasting oven). Remove the skin and any sinews from the chicken. Place in a food processor and process until finely minced. Add the eggs, season with some black pepper and process until evenly mixed. Then add the lemon juice, tarragon and parsley and process, slowly adding the cream. Season with salt to taste. Cover and chill until needed. Grease a 1.75 litre/3 pint terrine or loaf tin with the butter and line the base with a piece of greased greaseproof paper or non-stick silicone paper. Top and tail the French beans and trim the carrots. Blanch in two separate pans of boiling salted water for 5 minutes. Drain and rinse under cold running water. Carefully stir the green peppercorns into the chicken mixture.

Spoon a third of the chicken mixture into the terrine and spread evenly to cover the base. Lay the French beans on top, leaving a 1 cm/½ in border all the way around. Cover with half the remaining chicken mixture, levelling it carefully. Lay the carrots on top, again leaving a 1 cm/½ in border, and spread over the rest of the chicken mixture. Cover the terrine with a piece of buttered greaseproof paper and then cover with foil and place in a roasting tin. Pour in enough boiling water to come halfway up the sides of the terrine and bake for 40–45 minutes or until a skewer inserted into the centre comes out clean. Remove from the oven, leave to cool completely and chill until ready to serve.

Meanwhile, make the tomato sauce. Place the *sugo* in a bowl, stir in the herbs and add a pinch of sugar to taste. Season well and chill until ready to serve. When ready to serve, turn the terrine out on to a plate and wipe with kitchen paper to remove any butter or liquid. Cut into slices and serve with the tomato sauce.

Seafood Feuilletté

SERVES 14–16

This may be a very spectacular dish to behold but its very easy to make. Just begin with ready-made, vegetarian-style puff pastry and some ready-made French-style hollandaise sauce and trust me.

1.5 kg/3 lb haddock, skinned and boned
600 ml/1 pint full cream milk
2 × 225 g/8 oz packets of puff pastry, defrosted if frozen 🛒 (see page 142)
beaten egg, to glaze
50 g/2 oz softened butter
50 g/2 oz plain flour
1 tbsp Dijon mustard 🛒 (see page 15)
seasoning
275 ml/9 fl oz Hollandaise Sauce (bought or see recipe page 22)
450 g/1 lb white crab meat, defrosted if frozen

750 g/1½ lb large cooked peeled prawns, defrosted if frozen 🛒 (see page 57)
225 g/8 oz button mushrooms, thinly sliced
seasoning
Lemon and Almond Rice (see recipe page 206), to serve

Preheat the oven to 210C/425F/Gas 7/190C fan (top of the Aga roasting oven). Cut each piece of the haddock into 2–3 pieces and place in the milk. Poach over a moderate heat for 10 minutes until the fish is lightly cooked. Lift out the fish and reserve the milk. Flake the fish discarding any remaining skin and bone. Roll the puff pastry into two oblongs, about 1 cm/½ in thick. They should aim to be at least 30 cm/12 in long and 20 cm/8 in wide. Place them on two baking sheets (Swiss roll tins turned upside down are perfect), brush with beaten egg and bake for 15–20 minutes, until they are puffed up and golden.

Meanwhile, mix the butter, flour and mustard to a paste and add a little of the milk in which you have poached the haddock, then add the remaining milk and bring gently to the boil. Simmer for 2–3 minutes, stirring until it's a smooth sauce. Season to taste. Remove from the heat and stir in the hollandaise sauce. Stir in the crab meat, prawns, flaked haddock and mushrooms. Keep warm on a low heat or in a warming oven.

When ready to serve, split the puff pastry oblongs lengthwise, horizontally, as close to the top as possible. Remove any soggy flaky filling from the lower part of the oblong, leaving an edge around as a case. Do this with both oblongs. Bring the sauce to the boil for no more than 20 seconds. Spoon half the fish filling into the bottom of each pastry case and replace the lids. You can, if you wish, pop these back in the oven to brown a little more but it's unnecessary. To serve, cut into 3.5–4 cm/1½–2 in slices across and serve with a fish slice. Serve with the *Lemon and Almond Rice*.

FAR LEFT
Layered Chicken Terrine
(see page 202)

BELOW LEFT
Seafood Feuilletté
(see page 203)

RIGHT
Lemon and Almond Rice
(see page 206)

BELOW
Fruit Custard Brûlée
(see page 206)

Lemon and Almond Rice

SERVES 14–16

Good enough to eat on its own with some salad, this rice dish also makes the perfect accompaniment for the Seafood Feuilletté.

225 g/8 oz blanched almonds
675 g/1½ lb long-grain or basmati rice
2 tsp salt
25 g/1 oz fresh parsley
2 tbsp sunflower oil
50 g/2 oz butter
450 g/1 lb oyster or chestnut mushrooms
   (see page 66), washed and thinly sliced
grated rind and juice of 3 lemons
seasoning

Toast the almonds in a hot, dry, frying pan until they are golden brown. Remove from the pan and set them aside. Cook the rice in plenty of boiling water with the salt for 10–12 minutes until the rice is just cooked and tender. You will probably find it best to do this in 2 large pans rather than all at once in a huge one. Finely chop the parsley, discarding the stalks. Heat the oil and butter in 2 large frying pans and fry half the mushrooms in each for 2–3 minutes until they are a little softened. Add the almonds and rice to the pans and stir until the rice is warmed through. Add half the parsley, lemon rind and the juice to each pan and season to taste. Serve hot.

Fruit Custard Brûlée

SERVES 14–16

If you want to be ultra crafty with this recipe, you can buy fresh ready-prepared custard.

1 large pineapple
675 g/1½ lb seedless green grapes
900 ml/1½ pints thick Greek yoghurt
900 ml/1½ pints ready-made pouring custard
grated rind of 2 lemons
100 g/4 oz demerara sugar

With a sharp knife cut the pineapple in half lengthways. Lay the halves cut side up on a work surface and score the flesh of each pineapple with a noughts-and-crosses board of cubes about 1 cm/½ in square, cutting down to the skin but not right through. Cut a ring around the outside of the noughts-and-crosses board, but inside the skin of the pineapple, as though you were preparing a grapefruit, then with a strong spoon pop the cubes out into a bowl. Add the grapes and mix well. Preheat the grill. Place the fruit in the bottom of a shallow 3.5 litre/6 pint baking dish. Mix together the yoghurt, custard and lemon rind and spread over the fruit to cover it completely. Chill until ready to serve, then sprinkle over the sugar evenly and grill until bubbling. Serve at once. You can chill the brûlée again until ready to serve but you will lose the crunchiness of the caramel topping.

Crafty Tips

- You can prepare the *Layered Chicken Terrine* the day before (leave it to cool before chilling).
- The basic sauce could be made the day before without the seafood added. Leave to cool with a piece of lightly buttered greaseproof paper on top to prevent a skin forming, and chill.
- You could bake the pastry cases up to 4 hours in advance, ready to fill.

- The *Lemon and Almond Rice* can also be prepared up to 4 hours in advance. Simply cover with clingfilm and chill until ready to serve, then reheat either over a steamer or in a microwave. Alternatively you could just remove it from the fridge an hour before serving to allow it to come up to room temperature.

ENTERTAINING 30 PEOPLE

This menu is a buffet meal for a wedding or similar celebration that requires the feeding of the five thousand, so to speak. This particular menu has a Mediterranean feel to it. The first course is a selection of bruschetta (Italian bread-based savouries). It includes all sorts of grand combinations but none of them will break the bank.

For successful buffets it is essential that people can easily serve themselves from the individual dishes. So I've chosen an Italian-style chicken dish made from chicken breasts and some colourful vegetable skewers. There's also a vegetarian option with the *Tagliatelle and Artichoke Gratin*. This can accompany either of the other two main courses or be a main course in its own right. Two puddings complete this special feast which can be prepared entirely in advance.

Mixed Bruschetta Platter

SERVES 30 AS PART OF A BUFFET

A classic bruschetta is a simple affair of grilled bread, rubbed all over with garlic and brushed generously with extra-virgin olive oil. However, you can, of course, be more creative and top the toasts with all sorts of grand combinations. The flavours used here are all frequent partners, providing a selection of fabulous toppings.

2 plain ciabatta loaves
2 sun-dried tomato ciabatta loaves
2 olive ciabatta loaves
1 large garlic clove, peeled and halved
300 ml/½ pint extra-virgin olive oil 🛒
  (see page 15)
1 radicchio lettuce
1 tbsp red wine vinegar 🛒 (see page 16)
1 garlic clove, peeled and crushed
seasoning
15 slices bresaola 🛒 (see page 87)
25 g/1 oz Parmesan cheese shavings
10 plum tomatoes
2 × 50 g/2 oz cans anchovy fillets, drained
4 tbsp shredded basil leaves
6 tbsp ready-made pesto sauce 🛒
  (see page 33)
350 g/12 oz Fontina cheese
50 g/2 oz stuffed green olives

Preheat the grill and cut each ciabatta into 15 slices, discarding the ends. Toast the bread lightly on both sides and rub all over with garlic halves. Brush liberally with olive oil, reserving 4 tablespoons to use later, and set the bruschetta aside. Separate the radicchio into leaves, wash and pat dry with paper towels, then shred the lettuce and place in a bowl. To make the dressing, put the remaining oil in a screw-topped jar with the vinegar, and add seasoning. Shake to combine, pour over the radicchio and toss to coat all the leaves.

Top 30 of the plain slices of bruschetta with a small handful of the dressed leaves. Cut each slice of bresaola in half and roll each half into cigar shapes and place one on top of each plate. Garnish with Parmesan shavings. Slice the tomatoes and arrange 2–3 slices on each piece of sun-dried tomato bruschetta. Halve the anchovies and place 2 pieces in a criss-cross pattern on each one and garnish with shredded basil leaves. Spread the pesto on each piece of olive bruschetta. Slice the Fontina or cut into small cubes and arrange on top of the pesto. Garnish with the olives. These will sit in the fridge for up to 1 hour before serving.

Pollo Rosso

SERVES 30 AS PART OF A BUFFET

This is an Italian-style dish in the modern manner, cooked with the fashionable flavours of balsamic vinegar and sun-dried tomatoes.

30 × 75–100 g/3–4 oz chicken breast fillets, skinned
8 tbsp olive oil 🛒 **(see page 15)**
450 ml/¾ pint balsamic vinegar
10 garlic cloves, peeled and crushed
4 large sprigs of rosemary
2 × 165–190 g/5½–7 oz jars sun-dried tomato paste or condimento
1.5 litres/2½ pints water
seasoning

In 3–4 large frying pans, sauté the chicken breasts in the olive oil for 2–3 minutes a side until lightly golden. You could do this in batches and then place in one big pan. Carefully pour in the vinegar and stir all the crusty bits into the liquid. Add the garlic, rosemary and tomato paste or condimento. Turn the chicken to coat it well and add 300 ml/½ pint of water to each 6 chicken breasts. Simmer for 25 minutes or until the chicken is cooked through, spooning the sauce over it occasionally and turning it once. Season to taste – it may not need anything. This will keep warm if not overcooked in the first instance for up to 1 hour in a low oven, well covered.

But ensure that the chicken has been thoroughly reheated to a temperature above 70C/160F before serving (see 'Avoiding Food Poisoning', page 215).

Tagliatelle and Artichoke Gratin ⓥ

SERVES 30 AS PART OF A BUFFET

It's now possible to buy what used to be exotic ingredients like artichoke hearts in supermarkets and speciality food shops all over the country. This allows you to make dishes that used only to be available in Tuscan hills.

500 g/1¼ lb tagliatelle pasta
4 tbsp ready-made pesto sauce 🛒 **(see page 33)**
2 × 290 g/10 oz jars artichoke hearts preserved in oil
4 eggs
750 ml/1¼ pints double cream
75 g/3 oz freshly grated Parmesan cheese
seasoning

Preheat the oven to 200C/400F/Gas 6/180C fan (top of the Aga roasting oven). Cook the pasta in a large pan of boiling salted water for 3 minutes. Take off the heat and set aside with the lid on for 7–8 minutes until just tender and cooked through. Drain the pasta, return to the pan and toss with the pesto sauce. Leave to cool. Meanwhile, drain the artichoke hearts and roughly chop if this has not already been done. Mix together the eggs, cream, and 50 g/2 oz of the Parmesan until well combined. Add the artichoke hearts and egg mixture to the pasta and stir well to combine. Season to taste. Transfer to a 25 × 30 cm/10 × 12 in deep roasting tin and sprinkle over the remaining Parmesan. Bake for 25–30 minutes until just set and lightly golden. Serve hot.

Tagliatelle and Artichoke Gratin

LEFT
Crafty Tiramisu
(see page 214)

BELOW LEFT
Mediterranean Vegetable Skewers
(see page 212)

and Pollo Rosso
(see page 208)

BELOW
Mixed Bruschetta Platter
(see page 207)

Mediterranean Vegetable Skewers Ⓥ

SERVES 30 AS PART OF A BUFFET

Grilled vegetables are very fashionable at the moment in expensive restaurants. They are, however, extraordinarily easy to make.

2 small aubergines
3 yellow peppers
3 red onions
4 courgettes
350 g/12 oz cherry tomatoes
juice of 1 lemon
2 tsp clear honey
3 tbsp chopped fresh oregano
120 ml/4 fl oz olive oil 🛒 (see page 15)
seasoning

Soak 30 bamboo skewers in water to prevent them from burning. Cut the aubergine into 2.5 cm/1 in pieces. Cut the peppers in half, remove the seeds and cut each half into six pieces. Peel the onions, leaving the root intact, and cut each onion into eight wedges. Trim the courgettes and cut into 2.5 cm/1 in pieces. Preheat the grill. Mix together the lemon juice, honey, oregano, olive oil and seasoning and place in a large bowl. Add all the prepared vegetables with the tomatoes and toss to coat. Thread on to the 30 bamboo skewers. Place on to the grill rack and brush with any remaining oil mixture – you may have to do this in batches. Grill for 10–15 minutes, turning and brushing frequently. Serve warm or cold.

Peaches Baked in Honey and Lemon

SERVES 30 AS PART OF A BUFFET

This recipe takes, literally, minutes to prepare but only seems to last a couple of seconds at the table.

15 peaches or 4 × 400 g/14 oz cans peach halves in natural juice
8 cardamom pods 🛒 (see page 67)
50 g/2 oz sugar
6 tbsp clear honey
juice and rind of 2 lemons
150 ml/¼ pint white grape juice
crème fraîche 🛒 (see page 58), to serve

Preheat the oven to 200C/400F/Gas 6/180C fan (top of the Aga roasting oven). If using fresh peaches, place in a pan of boiling water and leave for 1 minute. Remove with a slotted spoon and drain on kitchen paper. Peel, cut in half and remove the stones. Arrange the fresh or canned peach halves in a large ovenproof dish. Lightly bruise the cardamom pods and scatter them around. To make the syrup, place the sugar, honey, lemon juice and rind in a small pan and add the grape juice. Bring to the boil and simmer for 1–2 minutes until the sugar has dissolved. Pour over the peach halves and bake for 20–25 minutes, basting occasionally. Serve at once with a bowl of crème fraîche or let the peaches cool in the syrup and serve cold.

Peaches Baked in Honey and Lemon

Crafty Tiramisu

SERVES 30 AS PART OF A BUFFET

Tiramisu has recently become an incredibly fashionable pudding. It's certainly for high days and holidays as it's formidably calorific but very delicious. The combination of sweet mascarpone cheese, and chocolate and coffee flavoured almond crunch is almost irresistible. It benefits from being stood for at least 1–2 hours so it's ideal, too, for a buffet like this as it can be made in advance.

3 eggs
3 × 250 g/9 oz tubs mascarpone cheese
150 g/5 oz thick Greek yoghurt
75 g/3 oz caster sugar
1½ tsp vanilla essence
30 amaretti biscuits 🛒
150 ml/¼ pint strong black coffee
50 g/2 oz plain chocolate, grated

Separate the eggs and mix the yolks with the mascarpone cheese and yoghurt to a smooth paste in a large bowl. Beat in the sugar and vanilla essence until the whole mixture is smooth and glossy. Whip the egg whites in a separate bowl until stiffened and fold into the mascarpone cheese mixture. Place the amaretti biscuits in a large bowl and pour over the strong black coffee and mix until all the biscuits are roughly crushed and well soaked. Put a layer of biscuits into a large glass bowl, then spoon over a layer of the mascarpone cheese mixture, put another layer of amaretti on top and finish with a layer of the mascarpone cheese mixture. Sprinkle the grated chocolate on top to cover completely. This will sit contentedly in the fridge for up to 6 hours. When serving, make sure that everybody gets a layer of the cream and the bitter coffee-flavoured biscuits to balance it.

AMARETTI BISCUITS
These small Italian biscuits are wrapped individually in coloured tissue paper and are made from almonds and/or the almond flavoured kernels of apricots and peaches. They are usually served with strong coffee after a meal but in this recipe they have the coffee added to them first. You can save money by buying the unwrapped biscuits for this recipe.

Crafty Tips

● Toast the ciabatta up to 24 hours in advance and store in an airtight container. You can also prepare the topping ingredients up to 1 hour in advance.

● The *Pollo Rosso* can be cooked completely the day before and reheated when ready to serve.

● The best way to get ahead on the *Tagliatelle and Artichoke Gratin*, up to 24 hours in advance, is to toss the cooked pasta in the pesto sauce and artichokes and place in the roasting tin. Allow to cool completely, then cover and chill. Mix together the eggs, cream, Parmesan and seasoning in a bowl, cover and chill, then when you are ready to cook simply pour the egg mixture over the flavoured pasta and bake as described.

● The *Mediterranean Vegetable Skewers* can be threaded on to their skewers and placed in a non-metallic dish. Drizzle over any remaining marinade and chill for up to 24 hours.

● The *Crafty Tiramisu* and the *Peaches Baked in Honey and Lemon* can also be made the day before and served straight from the fridge.

Avoiding Food Poisoning

Food poisoning is often an unwelcome addition to the menu at home-catered weddings. Food is prepared in advance, often left out in a warm room or marquee and things always run late. These are the perfect conditions for food poisoning bacteria (such as salmonella and campylobacter) to multiply rapidly in high risk foods like poultry and eggs. To avoid such a disastrous outcome observe a few simple rules.

Crucially:

If poultry is cooked for eating later, cool it as quickly as possible, then cover and refrigerate.

———

Keep cold dishes refrigerated until serving.

———

Ensure hot dishes are reheated thoroughly above 70C/160F before serving.

And bear these basic rules in mind when preparing the food:

Observe personal hygiene. Wash your hands before handling food and cover up cuts and sores with a plaster. Do not sneeze in the vicinity of food.

———

Keep cooked and raw foods separate to avoid cross-contamination.

———

Knives and other utensils must be washed between handling raw and cooked food.

———

Defrost frozen food thoroughly before cooking.

———

Keep pets away from food preparation surfaces and clean as you go using a disinfectant.

Wedding drinks

Although the main *substance* of a wedding feast is provided by the food, possibly an even more crucial (dare I say) part is played by the drink. People worry a lot about their wedding wine. It's important, and sets the tone of the occasion in a way.

The focal point of any wedding reception is the cake cutting, the speeches and the toasts, and, whatever the budget for booze may be, this tends to be the highspot in the glass. But the good news is that it's certainly not necessary to offer your 'toast' wine the party through. If you want to push the boat out and serve Champagne with the cake, it's perfectly possible (and perfectly chic) to offer a lesser alternative beforehand. So here I'm going to suggest medleys of wines and sparklers to suit most budgets. But let's look at that all important wine for the toast first.

SPARKLING WINE

The most traditional celebration wine has to be Champagne, and were money no object, that's what I'd go for; a mature, well-made Champagne. Since the process for retaining bubbles in wine was first 'discovered' by a monk in the Champagne region of France in the eighteenth century (when he declared at first sip 'I am drinking the stars') it's held centre stage as the most luxuriously festive drink. *But* Champagne is a single *appellation*, a single umbrella covering every single sparkling wine coming from the Champagne region north east of Paris. By no means are all Champagnes equally enjoyable. Which one should you choose?

Money is, of course, an important factor. Expensive champagne (such as Krug, my top of the pops, money aside) is exorbitantly expensive, and certainly not worth squandering on a big party. Well-known, mid-priced Champagnes, the big names such as Moët & Chandon and Veuve Cliquot, look impressive because they are instantly recognisable, but they, too, make a large dent in your budget. But if you step further down the price ladder you can very easily stumble into the sort of cheap Champagne that gives France a bad name; bottles costing £10 or so, which taste aggressively acidic, sharp and raw, are not worth the money and do not live up to their illustrious name.

Sometimes these disappointments are simply poor

INVISIBLE ECONOMIES

If you like the idea of sparkling wine, but your budget only runs to the cheapest, go for it, remembering you can cheer it up with an exotic additive. Crème de mûre is a delicious blackberry inspired liqueur (a little goes a very long way) and a dash of it in the bottom of the glass turns the wine an exotic violet shade, gives it an instant hedgerow scent and friendlifies it with sweet fruit. Crème de cassis is the blackcurrant equivalent, better known and a bit less exotic. You can find fruit syrups in imaginative wine shops, and these give the same sort of effect more cheaply, without the additional alcohol. Alternatively, cheer up cheap, dry white wine in the same way.

Champagnes, made from poor fruit from the worst parts of the designated region. Sometimes, though, they are all right underneath, just far too young for their own good. In either case, though, they can be improved upon simply by allowing them more time to mature. Since most weddings are planned quite far in advance, the months elapsing between engagement and wedding party can be put to good use 'improving' a cheap Champagne. As soon as you know you are planning a party, ask for the shop's recommendation of their best well-priced Champagne (or special offer); buy up what you need and find a cool dark place to store it in until the party. Six months, nine months, a year's storage will do the fizz nothing but good and make it taste twice the drink it was.

Or you could go for a sparkling wine from somewhere other than Champagne. Only a few years ago 'alternative' sparkling wines were seen as second best. But not any more. Magnificent sparklers are made all over the world, and 'New World' wine-making methods (coupled with really ripe fruit) have seen to it that they avoid all the sharpness of inexpensive, immature Champagne. Australia, New Zealand and South Africa are all now reliably supplying us with delicious sparkling wines with real class, tasting often much better than inexpensive Champagnes and even than the well-known brands. Some cost as much as the cheaper Champagnes (and frequently taste a lot more expensive), others shave a few pounds off the price and taste pretty good as well.

So if you're not hung up on the snobbery of the name Champagne you should simply pay what you can afford (giving Cavas from Spain and Saumurs from France a miss). Ten years ago this would have been ludicrous advice. Now happily you're quite safe to economise!

So far the assumption has been that your celebration fizz will be dry. But, but, but, there's no reason why it should be. The words Asti Spumante have not in the past been considered to be terribly chic, but things have changed considerably in the sweet wine department as well. Now Italian wines, both entirely fizzy like Asti and Moscato Spumante and only slightly so like Moscato Naturale have taken on a new lease of life. And what better accompaniment to the wedding cake? If you choose to serve a sparkling wine only to accompany the cake cutting and toasts, then a lusciously grapey-but-delicate Asti or Moscato is ideal.

HOW MUCH WINE TO BUY

For sparkling wine throughout the reception, allow ¾ of a bottle per head and ½ a bottle per head if orange juice is being offered as a mixer. For the toasts, allow one glass per head (allow 6 glasses per bottle). For wine to be served only until the toasts, buy 'sale or return' and allow ½ a bottle of white and ½ a bottle of red per head. For wine to be served throughout the party, including the toasts, again buy 'sale or return' and allow ¾ of a bottle of white and ½ a bottle of red per head. A lot should be left to be returned!

DO'S AND DON'TS

Do:
Chill all white wines thoroughly first. Since you are unlikely
to have enough fridge space, buy ice (many garages and off-
licences do it by the bag, or fishmongers can recommend
where you get it in blocks) and use the bath or clean buckets
or dustbins. Some wine shops even supply the bins themselves.

Don't:
Chill wines you buy on 'sale or return' on ice or it will
damage the labels and you'll be unable to return the bottles.

Do:
Offer plenty of soft alternatives. Orange juice is fine (the
better the quality, the better the taste) but get in stocks of
sparkling water too.

Don't:
Have spirits visibly on hand unless you are prepared to offer
them to everyone; if you have to give old Uncle Harold a
whisky, give it to him in a wine glass and tell him to keep
quiet.

Do:
Check – and sniff – each glass individually if you are
borrowing or hiring them. Frequently they have not been
washed up properly by the previous users and need another
wash.

Don't:
Skimp on the quantity of drink on offer. It's embarrassing
to run out so better to over cater on a 'sale or return' basis
or, after offering one or two drinks to your guests, you could
consider introducing a pay bar. If you are going to do this,
it's best, if possible, to indicate as much on the invitation. If
you are buying much more wine on 'sale or return' than
you expect to drink, keep some of it hidden and secure, to
be called on only if necessary. Make a note in advance how
much you have put aside so as to avoid any arguments as to
where it all went when the party really got going.

RECIPE INDEX BY COURSE

Page numbers in italics refer to the pictures.

INDEX

Page numbers in italics refer to the pictures.